JESUS TODAY
A Quaker Perspective

JESUS TODAY

A Quaker Perspective

Michael Wright

First published in paperback in 2019 by Sixth Element Publishing
on behalf of Michael Wright

Arthur Robinson House
13-14 The Green
Billingham TS23 1EU
Tel: 01642 360253
www.6epublishing.net

© Michael Wright 2019

ISBN 978-1-912218-57-8

British Library Cataloguing in Publication Data. A catalogue record for this
book is available from the British Library.

Printed in Great Britain.

CONTENTS

INTRODUCTION
WHAT'S THIS ALL ABOUT?

I have had a life-long respect and admiration for Jesus. These days I think so many people who might well share my respect for him, know hardly anything about him. The fresh knowledge provided by biblical scholars in the last fifty or more years passes most people by.

I have been encouraged by friends to share a little of my journey and experiences as an introduction to this book. It is written with Quakers in mind, many of whom these days know little about Jesus, even though the Religious Society of Friends (Quakers) in Britain is rooted in the Christian tradition and has always found inspiration in his life and teachings. I hope it may also be helpful to others, whether active church members or not, who are interested in a modern perspective on Jesus. I have been very much helped in writing this by consulting various friends who share some of my interests. As well as Quakers, they include Methodists, Anglicans and Roman Catholics. They have told me that what I have written will be of interest to some fellow members of the churches to which they belong.

I grew up in a household with no connections with religion. As a teenager at school I was something of an unwelcome presence in Religious Studies. I asked too many questions and I challenged what was taught. With the arrogant confidence of a teenager, I decided to research and show that religious beliefs were false. Whilst doing this, I was brought up short by an unexpected experience. Reflecting alone in my bedroom one summer evening, gazing out of the window, I had an overwhelming experience of love and joy and peace. The world seemed a very different place after this.

It was so overwhelming I became convinced God had caught up with me. Within a couple of years I began training for ordination in the Church of England. I was sent to a one-year access course in Durham, with thirty other young men, before my three years at Chichester Theological College. The Durham course was a deliberate ploy to put together men from the whole range of the Church of England from low church Evangelicals to high church Anglo-Catholics. Most of them spent a great deal of time discussing or arguing about doctrine and liturgy.

I felt somewhat lost, and wondered: "Is this what it is all about?" I found my way to Durham Quaker Meeting. It was an oasis of tranquillity, sanity and practical application of Christian values. Those Quakers were unable to help me much when I enquired of them about their doctrinal beliefs but they gave me a copy of their little booklet *Advices & Queries*. It impressed me deeply. It shaped my life and thinking over the following years of my Anglican ministry.

Nearly forty years later I was a Hospice Chaplain. With a lifetime of pastoral practice, reading, reflecting and exploring with others, my theological views had changed. I started again to go to my local Quaker Meeting and felt more at home there. I felt my views had changed too much to remain an official representative of the Church of England. I gave some months' notice that I wished no longer to hold episcopal permission to officiate and laid aside my Anglican ministry.

When I returned to Quaker Meetings for Worship after a gap of nearly forty years, I felt I was listening for a voice 'from the beyond'. I soon came to realise I was listening to a voice from within. Before long I had lost God and felt bereaved, but I knew that the Quaker meeting was the right place for me. In time I found some new ways of being Quaker without needing to focus either my loyalty or my spiritual practice on God.

In this book I share something of my perspective on Jesus and on Quaker practice, which I hope might be helpful, encouraging, even enlightening to others. Some members of churches find participation in Quaker Meetings is both fruitful and helpful. I know of several people who choose to have joint membership of their own church denomination and of the Religious Society of Friends. What I am seeking to share with those who read this is a fresh appreciation of Jesus, his life and teaching, which is not trapped in various mindsets of the past. I hope to encourage others to realise his significance for today. The person of Jesus, rather than the Christ of the creeds, attracts, challenges and encourages still, by the values, attitudes and practices that he inspires.

Not all British Friends value Jesus as central to our modern Quaker way. Few people refer to Jesus or the gospels in Meetings for Worship. Mention of him can even be unwelcome to some. I hope now to stimulate an interest in the significance of his teaching from which we can draw inspiration for our values and practice today. I would also like to stimulate an interest amongst Friends and others, to explore other books of the bible with a modern, intelligent, enquiring approach. Many Quakers and church members tend to refer to the bible very rarely. Many have little knowledge even of the gospels. Of those who learnt stories from the bible as children, few have updated their knowledge and understanding of its texts since then. The bible is a source of much that is central to our Quaker way and I find the variety of stories, teachings, poetry, visions, myths and personal experiences, all a rich treasure trove to inspire, encourage, challenge and enlighten me.

For more than twelve years I have organised a monthly Quaker-based ecumenical Book Club in our Area Meeting. In this group we have read and discussed a variety of modern writings about Jesus. Here I am seeking to share a view of how I see the application of his life and teaching as significant for us today. I hope we can again openly value him in our Meetings for Worship, as central to our tradition, and to modern British Quaker life and practice.

Friends who do cherish Jesus have a range of views and practices in relation to him. For some he is a remarkable prophet, whose words and actions are perhaps the finest flowering of the Jewish prophetic and wisdom literature and whose insights are much needed in the cultural turbulence of our times. For others, as he was for early Friends, he is the embodiment of the divine: an intimate companion in silent worship, a guide in the daily choices in life and a strength and comforter in times when life is difficult.

Some Friends find they move on the spectrum between these perspectives as circumstances, understandings and their needs suggest. Others hold fast to their experiences and convictions nurtured from childhood or from an experience which some describe as 'conversion' and others might call 'transformation'.

In taking this look at Jesus, I want to portray him in language which I hope will connect to those unfamiliar with him in the first place or whose familiarity with him has faded over the years. I hope all of us can respect the views and experiences of those which are different from our own and that we can learn from each other.

I trust readers who are familiar with the bible will not find some of my basic explanations at times too elementary. I have become aware that some people will come to this material entirely fresh, with no previous knowledge of the bible. I hope to stimulate people to delve into the wisdom of Jesus, look at the background to his teaching and some of the fruits of it elsewhere in the New Testament. Maybe some might even venture to discover much that they value in the Old Testament too.

Advices & Queries: The quotations in italic print in this book are all from the small booklet available in any Quaker Meeting, *Advices & Queries*. The present edition of them has changed twice since I first encountered them in 1959. To me they are the central focus of our Quaker way.

Quaker faith & practice: This is the Book of Discipline of the Religious Society of Friends (Quakers) in Britain that I quote from in several places. It has been compiled after much deliberation throughout our Society. It contains guidance on best practice for church government, and the responsibilities of people who serve in various capacities in local and area meetings, and on national committees. It is also a collection of examples of the experiences of many Quakers since the earliest days in the 1650s of their insights, experiences and their encouragement to others. It is currently undergoing a revision which will take some years to complete.

The New Testament: I recommend readers who may be

prompted by this book to explore the New Testament for the first time, or to revisit it after a long gap, to purchase a copy of the *Revised New Jerusalem Bible (New Testament and Psalms)* – Darton, Longman & Todd 2018. This revised text, in modern appropriate language, with gender parity, has helpful introductory notes to each book, and notes on particular references throughout.

In Friendship
Michael Wright

CHAPTER 1
A FRESH ENGAGEMENT WITH JESUS

*The Religious Society of Friends is rooted in
Christianity and has always found inspiration
in the life and teachings of Jesus.
Advices & queries 4.*

It was a fresh engagement with Jesus that transformed the lives of George Fox and other early Friends, though they all tended to focus on the post-Easter Christ rather than the pre-Easter Jesus. Fox searched for years, longing for a religious understanding and experience which would satisfy his need. It seems the preachers of his day, whether in the parish churches or in the independent congregations, were long on doctrine and short on helping their listeners to a personal spiritual engagement with Jesus.

Fox later dictated his Journal and recorded: "And when all my hopes in them [the priests and the separate preachers] and in all men were gone so that I had nothing outwardly to help me, nor could tell what to do, then, oh then, I heard a voice which said, 'There is one, even Christ Jesus, that can speak to thy condition', and when I heard it my heart did leap for joy'." He continued, "And this I knew experimentally"[1] – that is by experience.

When Fox had grown in confidence and conviction,

he began to share his experience and understanding of what Jesus taught to his disciples with others in groups, church congregations and other meetings. Many of those who heard him chose to join together to share Fox's vision and follow his way. They at first called themselves 'Seekers after Truth'. Within a short time they became the Society of Friends.

People have related and still do relate to Jesus in many different ways. He is a complex character and his role in history is complex too. In the past I have followed him as the divine Saviour: now I relate to him as a wise teacher. He is an inspiring figure who challenges, encourages and motivates me in seeking to live in something of the light that he has ignited in me. As our Quaker way is *"rooted in Christianity and has always found inspiration in the life and teachings of Jesus"* it would seem to be important for each of us to consider, as that Query asks *"How does Jesus speak to you today?"*

An understanding of who Jesus was, and what the authors of the four New Testament gospels were seeking to convey about him, has changed a very great deal in the last hundred years. Sadly, much of this knowledge is not widely disseminated in church congregations or in Quaker meetings. For many, he remains as portrayed in so many hymns, liturgies, crucifixes and paintings.

I wonder if Jesus is often seen by people who otherwise take little notice of him as more of a caricature than a real person. He may be a familiar name but he is largely unknown: a pasteboard figure preserved for some in the literary style of the King James version of the bible. He is more a stained-glass image than a man of life, energy, courage, feeling, imagination and power.

For many people he is a focus of worship and prayer – the Christ figure: a divine being, sinless, now living in heavenly glory. He is portrayed so often inside and outside many Anglican and Catholic churches nailed to a cross, gaunt, semi-naked and dead. This is far from the vital man he was in his prime. In such depictions he looks so very different from us that fewer and fewer people find him a person who inspires them, motivates them, challenges them or encourages them in their choices in everyday life. I suggest a fresh look at who Jesus was, what he taught, and how we understand his place in history, can refresh our vision of how our life and values today can be transformed in the modern world.

Modern knowledge from disciplines such as biblical studies and different theological approaches such as feminist and liberation theology, help us to encounter Jesus as a remarkably imaginative and creative teacher. From other disciplines such as archaeology, history, sociology and psychology, we learn a great deal more.

He was a deeply spiritual poet. He was a healer. He was a challenging and engaging preacher who was so different from the usual preachers and teachers of his day. He was a convivial man, who engaged in social contact with other people. He accepted their hospitality and cared deeply for their well-being. The gospels portray him as one who had a particular concern for those who were hungry, thirsty, poor, refugees, sick, imprisoned or otherwise oppressed.[2]

Jesus was an outstanding individual. He made an enormous impression on those who saw him in action relating to people and practising healing amongst them. What they heard him say was really radical and challenging. It was vivid. He had an unusual and distinctive view of the religious teachings of the Hebrew culture and how to apply them in daily life. He has remained a powerful influence for many millions of people over the more than two thousand centuries since his time.

His teaching is humane, caring and pastorally sensitive. He was clearly empathic and intuitive. He was also bluntly critical of hypocrisy, selfishness, financial dishonesty and double-dealing. He readily reached out to welcome those who were outcasts in society. He encouraged them to change their mindsets and to live with a loving attitude towards others. He had an openness to people and a concern for truth and integrity. He appears to have lived simply and cherished the natural world. He valued engagement both with people, and with the life of the spirit, from which he drew strength, vision and inspiration.

He engaged his quick mind and acute intelligence in debate with perceptive responses to those who opposed him. He was no fool. He took on the clever religious and legal people of his day with confidence. He used imaginative stories, each of which made a significant point vividly memorable. Whenever religious officials or lawyers tried to trap him, he confounded them.

This he did when they brought a woman caught in the act of adultery to him. The penalty for the woman was to be stoned to death! Jesus invited those who brought her to him, who were sure they themselves were without sin, to throw the first stone at her. One by one her accusers drifted away, leaving no one to accuse her. Jesus said he did not condemn her, but he encouraged her to make some changes in her life.[3]

When some Pharisees tried to trap him about the contentious issue of whether it was lawful according to the Jewish religious law to pay the Roman taxes or not, he asked to them to show him the coin required to pay the tax. It had the head of the Emperor on it. He replied, "Pay Caesar what belongs to Caesar and God what belongs to God."[4]

He challenged the hypocrisy of those who declared themselves religious but lacked the willingness to let compassion, empathy and care for others shape their understanding of life and its obligations. He made a towering indictment of religious hypocrisy.[5]

He was a man of great courage, prepared to act whilst well aware that the consequences of his words and actions could lead to the horrors of crucifixion: nailed by his hands and feet and lifted aloft to die very slowly and agonisingly. I see representations of his impaled figure so often that I can easily become inured to the full awfulness of that dreadful execution.

He seems to have been unusual in his dealings with women. He readily engaged in conversation with some whom he had not previously met. In John's gospel he is portrayed meeting a woman at a public well. There are just the two of them. Normal custom would allow minimal contact or conversation between them. He has a prolonged conversation with her. Even more shocking was the fact that he was a Jew, she was a Samaritan. The two races normally shunned each other.[6] He was also supported by a group of women, financially and practically, during his teaching journeys through Galilee.[7] In behaving like this, Jesus broke the strict practice of his culture yet he coped confidently with the opprobrium poured upon him because of doing so.

Cultural differences may well hide from us aspects of his Jewish sense of humour. Among things he picked up on was the contrast between one person who will criticise another's faults but cannot recognise their own. He compared such a person to a man who wants to remove a tiny speck from the eye of another but fails to realise he has an enormous plank sticking out of his own. This image strikes me as very like a modern satirical cartoon.[8]

I wonder if another example is his declaration that it is easier for a camel to pass through the eye of a needle than for a rich man to get into heaven. Was this something of a memorable joke? Was it perhaps a reference to a well-known narrow gate in Jerusalem that drivers had to unload their camels to get through? Did it have a local meaning for those he spoke to which is hidden from us today?[9] I just wonder what that was all about.

I am not alone in thinking that there is a significant contrast between Jesus' original teaching and behaviour and the authoritative doctrines and orthodoxies later developed and then imposed by the institutional churches. Quakers have largely either challenged or sidelined these since the foundation of our movement in the 17th century.

There is a wide range of views of Jesus amongst modern scholars who have studied his life and times. Some regard him as the last in a long line of prophets who laid the ethical and inspirational framework of Judaism – Moses, Elijah, Elisha, Isaiah, Jeremiah, Amos, Hosea and many others. Some who have examined in depth the history and theology of the Old Testament argue that Jesus saw himself as a prophet with a profound message from God. This was to warn his people of the end-time and the fulfilment of God's destiny of Israel.

Many people who know little or nothing about the scholarship relating to Jesus respond to him as they find him in the gospels. While some may be indifferent to him, for others he is a religious teacher whose words and actions inspire them. They may feel they can commune with him in times of quiet and prayer. He encourages and motivates people the world over to actions of loving concern for others. This may be for those close to them but often includes the wider community. They are drawn to acts of compassion, care and service to people they don't know because of their engagement with Jesus.

Quaker faith & practice[10] includes quotations from Friends in modern times for whom Jesus was central to their Quaker experience. "Brought up in a house where Jesus Christ was loved and honoured, I can never remember a time when his claims on me were not more or less a living issue," wrote J. Rowntree Gillett.[11] Others have shared a similar relationship with Jesus.

Frederick Parker-Rhodes answered the question, "Who is my God?" with "He speaks within me: if I mishear, my friends correct me: if I misdo, I look to Jesus Christ".[12] Hugh Doncaster wrote: "…this universal spirit is focused and made personal in Jesus in a way which makes it appropriate to speak of the Universal Light as the Light of Christ."[13] Janet Scott wrote: "We can respond to the Christ-event in such a way that we see Jesus as a symbol of God, a concrete example of divine being and action."[14] Paul Oestreicher wrote: "It is through him [Jesus] that I recognise God in my neighbour – through Jesus I've discovered the uniqueness of everyone."[15]

Jesus had spiritual strength and great self-confidence. He exercised this in a life of teaching and healing that astonished the crowds of people who flocked to him.[16] He drew that inner strength from the time he spent alone in prayer and contemplation.[17] He was a man with a deep trust in his relationship with God with whom he found a close intimacy.

Jesus' teachings urge people to make a revolution in the way we live and care for one another in society. He asks those who follow him to reflect deeply on our relationships with each other and to value a sense of the 'beyond'. Some modern versions of Christianity have reshaped his teaching and that of later Christian thinkers, largely by narrowing it to the key idea that it is Jesus' death on the cross and our hope of a heavenly afterlife that is what really matters.

Evangelical Christianity has sometimes had a profound effect in caring for the poorest and most vulnerable in society, for the homeless, the hungry, the migrants and asylum seekers. People who respond to the invitation to commit their lives to Jesus usually radically change their behaviour. Such commitment is able to bring about transformative changes in those hitherto without hope, including those addicted to a variety of substances and behaviours. Such faith shines as a light in dark places. The obverse side of such experiences can be that people find themselves directed by pastors, church elders and fellow worshippers in what to think, read and do in ways which some of them come to find restrictive and oppressive.

I can admire the commitment and the care that such faith evinces but I do not share it. My experience of life leaves me with no confidence in a life after death. Trusting that Jesus' death on the cross has somehow opened the way for those who accept Jesus as their Saviour to go to heaven when they die, leaves me unmoved.

I follow Jesus along a different path. This is the way that draws many of its features from the Quaker inheritance handed down from the first Friends. It has been developed and reshaped over more than three centuries of Quaker witness. As I understand this Quaker way, it has cherished Jesus as the Christ – has been inspired by him as a person, and valued his teaching and example as a way of living fully and lovingly. It has cherished the Light which as John's gospel declares is "the true light to everyone,"[18] which we understand to mean people the world over of all faiths and none.

This does not necessarily require us to understand things in exactly the same ways that previous generations have done. Many of us are willing to explore this experience of mystery and a spiritual life which is life-enhancing while prepared to consider that what we mean by 'God' is open to a variety of understandings, interpretations and descriptions.

The German theologian Rudolf Bultmann argued that the message of the New Testament had for too long been 'imprisoned' in the mythological worldview of Jesus' time. Bultmann called for a radical reinterpretation of this worldview, to fit our modern knowledge and understanding.

An example of this radical reinterpretation is offered by John Spong, a retired bishop of the American Episcopal church in his book *Unbelievable*. He writes of the impact that new knowledge had on the Christian view of the origin and development of life after Charles Darwin published his book *On the Origin of Species* in 1859.[19] The first three chapters of the bible contain the story of Adam and Eve who are living in a state of grace and without sin. Then they disobeyed God. Their sin, called their 'fall', led to them being ejected from God's Garden of Eden.

Spong writes:

"For Darwin creation was an ongoing, never-to-be-finished, evolutionary process. Human beings were thus forced to draw some radically new conclusions. Without an 'original perfection' in creation itself, there could not have been a fall from perfection into something that was called 'original sin'. If we did not fall into 'original sin' by an act of wilful disobedience, there was no need to be baptised 'for the remission of sin'. This meant that the story of God sending Jesus or incarnating the divine person in the human Jesus to overcome 'the fall', or to 'die for our sins', was reduced to little more than pious nonsense. Everywhere we looked, the traditional religious patterns began to fall into disuse." [20]

Such a radical challenge to traditional thinking inspired another German biblical scholar and theologian, Paul Tillich, to argue that when we envisage God what we mean is all that concerns us most deeply. He described God as "being itself" or "the ground of our being".

This may sound strange when we first encounter such an idea but it is not new. Reza Aslan in his book *God - a human history* describes the development of ideas and practices of human understanding of 'God' from the very earliest depictions to the present, over a period of about six million years. These have changed from a multitude of gods with very human characteristics to a single great god: from manifestations of the one god in various forms (as in the Hindu tradition) to a practice that takes no notice of any god (Buddhism). These ideas have also developed from tribal gods to a god who created all that exists, who chose the Jewish people for a special relationship. This God became the God of the Christians and of the Muslims. Aslan explores the various explanations for the divine, which include the anthropomorphic concept of God we have inherited. He ends with a focus on the soul:

"However you define it, belief in the soul as separate from the body is universal. It is our first belief, far older than our belief in God. It is the belief that begat our belief in God." [21]

The idea that our engagement with 'the divine' might be not so much with a heavenly father but with life itself, may be a 'light-bulb moment' or it may be difficult to grasp at first. Spong offers us his view of what this might mean in our experience of life and of love. The quotation below is just a part of his explanation of this idea.

"Love is the meaning of life we give to another. None of us can create love. None of us can give love until we have received it. So love is also a reality that relates us to something beyond ourselves. That is the meaning of transcendence.

Love however, is never disembodied, never found or experienced apart from life. Love passes through us... It must be shared or it will die. So love opens each of us to a dimension of the human experience that is transcendent. Love relates us to something that is real, but something that we can neither create nor destroy. God is the name by which we call this experience of love. If God is love, the only way we can worship God is by loving others. The more we give love away, the more we make the experience of God visible. God is not a being, external to us; God is experienced in the presence of love. God is the dimension of transcendence flowing through us... These ideas flow readily into the suggestion that God is not a being, but

'Being itself'. God is the Ground of Being in which our being is rooted... The more deeply and fully we can be ourselves, the more God, who is Being, becomes visible. The missionary thrust of this understanding can never be 'to convert the heathen'; it can only be to enhance the being of others, to give life to others and to enhance love in others."[22]

The traditional and familiar concept of an eternal father God located somewhere in the ethereal 'beyond' is one that no longer inspires love and loyalty for many of us, nor do we find it meaningful. We search for new ways of describing our experiences and our understanding.

We are challenged not to think of God as a being external to ourselves. Thomas Aquinas, the classic Catholic theologian of the 13th century, stated that God does not exist in the same way that anything we know of can be said to exist. The eastern Orthodox church teaches the 'apophatic' tradition as it is called: a theology of negatives. It states that we can only say what God is not, not what God is, for God is beyond any human conception.

Some people find the word 'God' still expresses very well all they mean by their experience of the divine. Others find that word so encumbered by baggage and associations of a frightening, controlling critical presence and mixed reactions to the masculine concept of 'father' that it is deeply unhelpful.

Jesus referred to God as 'Abba' – 'Father'.[23] This is how

Christians have mostly thought of God. We are inclined to think in terms of what we know, and so we find it natural to think of a relationship with an 'Other' in terms of human life. This has meant that a popular concept of God has become something too much like a super human being. The language of 'Father' and 'Son' is there in many prayers and hymns. It has tended to reinforce assumptions which worshippers rarely examine critically. Such notions have led so many people to think of God as 'Father' which is an anthropomorphic concept. This complicates things for us as we try to articulate our understanding of our spiritual experiences.

The familiar and traditional idea of God engages fewer and fewer of us today. Some different ways of describing what we may mean by 'God' may be helpful to people who are prepared to make a radical change in thinking. However, whatever our thinking and understanding about 'God', many of us find it important to engage in practices that feed our spirit: being still, waiting and listening to the 'spirit', personal self-examination, discernment, wonder, awe, thankfulness, seeking to nurture love in ourselves and others.

None of these necessarily require a focus directed at a precisely articulated concept of what we mean by 'God'. Quakers have long valued 'Light', 'Spirit', 'Leadings', 'Insight', as helpful words to convey something of the mystery we experience in our spiritual practices. We struggle to find words for that which is beyond words.

CHAPTER 2
GROWING IN LIGHT AND LOVE

Seek to know an inward stillness,
even amid the activities of daily life.
Advices & Queries 3.

Quakers are encouraged to find a way into silence which enables us to deepen our awareness of the divine and to find the inward source of our strength. This 'inward stillness' was a strong element in Jesus' life.

The first three gospels all record Jesus, immediately after his baptism by John in the river Jordan, retreating into the wilderness (an area of rough ground and rocky hills in Palestine) to be alone and still. Matthew and Luke write vividly of his 'temptations'.[1] Both of them present his ruminations to examine the dilemmas he faced in what today we might call a psycho-drama.

Modern psycho-drama uses guided dramatic action to help a person consider choices and actions facing them. It aims to develop insight and personal growth. It helps to integrate thinking, feelings and actions, to identify issues and to help personal well-being. It can give clarity to the choices an individual has to face.

Jesus was facing his own dilemmas. The gospels of both Matthew and Luke, in the culture of their time, present him facing them as a conversation with the devil. The time-span of 'forty days and forty nights' was a colloquial expression for a prolonged stay. It is not to be taken literally as a precise period of time. What it amounts to is that Jesus goes on retreat as he wonders how to present his message to the public.

Neither Matthew nor Luke could have been eye-witnesses nor listeners-in to Jesus' experience. He was alone. He may have talked some time later of his dilemmas and how he resolved them which both Matthew and Luke have presented in this very vivid way as temptations by the devil with flying visits to different venues! On the other hand, it may have been a tradition that grew up within the Christian community that he must have faced dilemmas like these and this is how some creative persons chose to depict him dealing with them.

The challenge to turn stones into bread could be a vivid way of articulating whether or not he is going to focus on meeting peoples' material needs. He opts not to. The challenge to worship the devil features as if he was tempted to seek political power, to be a national hero, the leader of a revolutionary movement. He turned this down. The third issue he faced was about doing spectacular things to make people notice him. He chose none of these as the style of his ministry. These temptations could be an invitation to engage with doubt: "**If** you are the Son of God…" – why not prove it to yourself at least? They are so rich in potential meanings that we can all find different layers and meanings in just such apparently simple stories. As his ministry develops, Mark depicts Jesus as needing his batteries recharged. He reports: "In the morning, while it was still deep in the night, he went out and left the house and went off to a lonely place and prayed there."[2] Later on, before he faced the ordeal of his trial and crucifixion, Jesus prayed alone in the Garden of Gethsemane.[3]

Mark also writes that Jesus said to his disciples, "'Come away by yourselves on your own to some lonely place and rest for a while', for there were so many coming and going that they had no leisure even to eat."[4] Jesus urged them to pray in private rather than publicly, doing so very simply, with love and trust.[5]

Other passages in the bible beloved of Quakers, include the prophet Elijah's experience on Mount Horeb, when he was escaping from the forces of Queen Jezebel. She wanted him killed. He was told to expect to encounter God on the mountain. So he waited, and first he endured a hurricane – but didn't experience God in that. Then came a fire – but God was not in that either. Next there was an earthquake – but God was not in that. After the earthquake came what is traditionally translated as "a still small voice". A modern translation has it as "the sound of sheer silence".[6] Yes, he found God in that sound of sheer silence – or if you prefer it "the still small voice".

Yet another passage treasured by Quakers is in the Revelation of John "...there was silence in heaven for about half an hour."[7] Seeking an inner stillness is a crucial element of the Quaker way. George Fox advised Oliver Cromwell's daughter Elizabeth Claypole in 1658: "Be still and cool in thy own mind and spirit from thy own thoughts, and then thou wilt receive his strength and power from whence life comes, to allay all tempests, against blusterings and storms. That is it which moulds up into patience, into innocency, into soberness, into stillness, into stayedness, into quietness, up to God, with his power".[8]

Meeting for Worship

Quaker Meeting for Worship, the shared practice of being still, in both body and mind, in a waiting and listening attitude, is the basic activity of our spiritual life. As we wait, we seek to be open, to listen to whatever may come to us. Sometimes that is simply refreshment, a relief from the busyness of everyday life. It may be nothing more than that but nevertheless very valuable in itself. As William Penn wrote in 1699, "True silence is the rest of the mind; and is to the spirit what sleep is to the body, nourishment and refreshment."[9]

At times, after a Meeting for Worship, we may find that we have renewed energy for everyday affairs, that our mind is clearer, perhaps our motivation for action is stronger. Some creative ideas or practice may develop in the following days or we come to have a change of attitude towards something or someone. It may well produce fresh insight and understanding about ourselves, our motives and behaviour.

Sometimes we find our thoughts leading in an unexpected direction and we follow that leading. We may find ourselves nourished and supported by the gathered community whether in sorrow or joy, or in dealing with a dilemma. There may also be times when we feel absolutely nothing and wonder if it has been a pointless exercise. It can be disheartening to have a succession of experiences like this. However, when something changes, either in our meeting or in ourselves and we experience something of the best that a Quaker gathered meeting can be, then we know we have 'a pearl of great price'.

Such experiences can be emotionally uplifting, inspiring, and enabling. Friends traditionally have trusted them to come from beyond us, a divine gift, an invitation to love and serve, with gifts of grace to enable us to do so.

Today, many Friends regard them more prosaically. The experience is valued, its fruits treasured, but what it is, or where it comes from, we are prepared to accept is a mystery. Others say they are the natural fruits of doing what few people choose to engage in: to be still together in a shared silence, waiting for insight, clarity, or creative change within ourselves or in other members of our meeting. Doing this is quite likely to produce such outcomes. Quaker Meetings for Worship, at their best, are deep wells of silence which have the potential to have a profound impression on those who share in them. Such meetings are commonly described as 'settled meetings'. At other times, where there is busyness about, it is more difficult to listen, to be open and attentive to what we might otherwise receive in silence.

It can be disappointing to be at a meeting and even more at a succession of meetings, that are not settled and from which we seem to give or gain little at all. There may be opportunities to raise our concerns with Elders or other Friends and to see whether some opportunities for sharing our stories or having a Woodbrooke-on-the-Road workshop might help to explore ways to deepen our meeting experiences. We are encouraged to: *Attend to what love requires of you, which may not be great busyness.*[10] This may mean a challenge to find ways of enriching love within ourselves towards other people.

The name 'Meeting for Worship' is something of a puzzle to a number of Friends. Who or what do we 'worship'? Meeting for Worship is the traditional name for this activity, and Friends trusted that as they offered themselves to listen to the Inward Teacher, they were offering service – worship – to God. If not all of us feel that is not what we are there to do, why do we continue to describe it as 'Meeting for Worship'? Quakers are largely very attached to traditional names for roles or activities which have long outlived their original designation: 'Meeting for Sufferings', 'Elders', 'Overseers' and 'testimony' are some examples of such archaic 'Quaker-speak'.

We are encouraged to consider the Quaker understanding of what we do when we gather together for Meeting for Worship in these words in *Advices & Queries: Worship is our response to an awareness of God. We can worship alone, but when we join with others in expectant waiting we may discover a deeper sense of God's presence. We seek a gathered stillness in our meetings for worship so that all may feel the power of God's love drawing us together and leading us.*[11]

The Shorter Oxford English Dictionary explains that the word worship comes from the Old English for worth, and so worth-ship. I can feel entirely relaxed and in no way hypocritical, about turning up each Sunday morning at my local Meeting House for an activity which is well worth doing. I may feel a power of love drawing members of the meeting together and aware sometimes of leadings. It can seem uncanny when one Friend speaks, then another (or more than one) finds those words relate closely to what has been in their minds in the same meeting but not verbalised until then.

In her book *Discernment and Inner Knowing* Joycelin Dawes, an established writer on Quaker and contemporary spirituality writes:

"Conventional images of God are increasingly replaced by connection with a deep source in an encounter that may be profound and transformative… This highlights the difference between taking a phrase, such as 'following the will of God' literally, and understanding it as a metaphor. However God is imagined, following the will of God may be perceived as a metaphor that points towards our interaction with source, a relationship with our deepest inner place; for many this is transcendent... Some of us stay in a framework of belief over a lifetime, for some it is more fluid and changeable... this is reflected for example in the difficulty many Quakers have in speaking about the nature of the source from which they act." [12]

I am content to let the origin of such experiences remain a mystery. Whether they are examples of mental telepathy that we hardly understand, or they are indeed promptings from a divine source, I am content to leave open. I am a Quaker. I share Quaker experiences. I value Quaker practices. I do not feel obliged to subscribe to philosophical speculations about the source of those experiences.

The key theme of the Quaker way seems to me to nourish and promote love. We find that love can flourish in us as we explore the light we encounter in the silence and fellowship of Quaker meetings at their best. Love does not flourish unless we relate lovingly to other people. That is surely why Jesus chose to invite people such as his twelve disciples and the women who supported him, to be close to him as he travelled through the countryside of Palestine teaching them a way of living that is focused on loving relationships. In time, his followers came to be known as 'People of the Way'. [13]

We see in the gospels many instances of Jesus in the company of his closest followers, women as well as men, among the large crowds who flocked to him. We find him sharing meals, visiting friends, encouraging and chastening them, teaching and telling stories. At times he is challenged by opponents. Sometimes his family and friends are protective and at other times they are critical of him. Relationships with other people were crucial to him and his way.

Fox and his friends also formed communities of Friends who would support and encourage one another in the Quaker way. I find myself affirmed in this way simply by regularly being present at Quaker meetings for worship, whether the event seems spiritually or emotionally significant or whether I learn anything new or not. Being with Friends affirms me in being Quaker.

This way is not individual but corporate, subject to the discipline, support and guidance of other members of the Society to which we belong. We are wise to step back from any course of action we may feel to be right, without the considered support of our Friends after we have properly consulted with them in a Meeting for Worship for Business, or have tested the course of action in either a Meeting for Threshing, or a Meeting for Clearness. Both of these meetings can be enormously helpful in exploring ideas and options, and finding appropriate forms of action.

We are indeed a Society of Friends. In the past Quakers were known as 'Friends of Truth' and 'Children of the Light'. Now our official title is The Religious Society of Friends (Quakers) in Britain. No society, group or association that does not change and adapt to new circumstances will long survive – they ossify. As the ways in which people have sought to follow the teaching of Jesus have changed in many different ways over more than 2,000 years, so our Society continues to be changed by its members, our experiences and convictions and the challenges we face.

Still and cool

I find it important to explore the riches of Fox's advice about being still and cool in our minds, through taking time to be still quite apart from when I am at a Quaker meeting. An Australian medical researcher, Ramesh Manocha, has written about his research into 'mind emptying' in his book *Silence Your Mind*.[14] In chapter five he provides some modern insights into practices common for centuries in religious disciplines. He has helped me appreciate the value of what can be gained from exploring silence with a mind that is empty of thoughts or images, but alert and focused.

His diagrams show what he describes as our normal, or usual, mental activity. This he depicts as a wavy line: it goes up and down, endlessly. When at leisure, our thoughts leap all over the place, like a group of monkeys ever busy, flitting hither and thither, even when we sometimes try to concentrate on one thing at a time. When we are doing several activities at once, these wavy thought-lines become busier than ever. When we are stressed, they increase dramatically, even frantically! Manocha teaches the importance of physical relaxation which can reduce the stimulation to the brain and allows the rate of thinking to slow. His research shows a link between slower thought-waves and improved mood. It may also stimulate creative activity, lead us to make wiser decisions and improve our whole attitude to life.

Further diagrams demonstrate small gaps between our thoughts as we relax and are calm. He is convinced most of us can learn gradually to lengthen these small gaps and so increase our mental silence. As we begin to do so, we teach ourselves to increase the space between our thoughts, until the gaps are longer than the thought periods. With further practice we can find fewer episodes of thought separated by longer periods of absence of thought – the silence of the mind.

Modern research technology can now show the changes in us when we do this. There are chemical changes, and the electrical signals associated with thinking are reduced. Mindfulness methods may also help us to reach that point of being able to still our minds and then to empty them. In that state, we are fully aware but without any thinking activity: this is mental silence. Manocha's book helped me to understand and develop this practice. It is something that I can use both alone and for some periods in a Quaker meeting. The value of such a practice has grown on me over time.

This seems to be a modern version of what George Fox found for himself and encouraged Elizabeth Claypole to discover. It has clarified for me the value of simply being still, of having periods of no thoughts, neither words nor pictures in my mind. The stillness of the body assists the stillness of the mind. Its benefits, both in a group or when alone, may well come later. It is the foundation of the method of being open, aware, in listening mode, receptive to whatever may come to us.

Spiritual practice

We are aware these days of a wide variety of spiritual practice, religious and secular, which can feed our souls. Our Quaker practice is part of this spectrum. As Philip Sheldrake explains in his *Spirituality – a very short introduction*,[15]

"Thus, rather than simply being one element among others in human existence, 'the spiritual' is best understood as the integrating factor – 'life as a whole'. Then spirituality is also understood to be engaged with a quest for the 'sacred'. This includes beliefs about God but also refers more broadly to the numinous, the depths of human existence, or the boundless mysteries of the cosmos."

Nowadays this may involve psychology, philosophy and sociology, not just theology or religious studies.

I like the phrase 'soul-silence' in Brian Holley's Kindlers booklet *Why Silence?*[16] He writes:

"By 'soul' I'm simply referring to something that is primarily inner, not something that goes to heaven when we die. Little is said about this profound level of silence, even in Quaker circles... Whether we refer to this experience as 'divine', 'soul', 'spirit', 'alternative consciousness' or even 'God' makes no difference to the experience... Spiritual language is largely expressed in metaphors and approximations because language is so inadequate in this sphere. It is the experience that counts."

Exploring 'soul-silence' he warns can result in increased compassion: it can transform us and all our relationships – so beware – we can expect to be changed by exploring it. Quaker Books publish a very helpful guide to resources for spiritual practice – *Deepening the life of the Spirit* developed by Ginny Wall.[17] I can warmly recommend this collection: I would expect anyone to find something in it that will be helpful in seeking to be 'still and cool' in mind and spirit. A shorter version is to be found in Appendix 1 of the Woodbrooke course *Becoming Friends*.[18] A copy of this course may well be in your local Meeting House library.

Those who study religious experiences, find that the

personal engagement with that mysterious Other tends to be more pronounced either when our brains are stimulated by people in a crowd that is moved and excited, or when our brains are resting in quietness and stillness. The first often happens in churches with singing, preaching or praying. The second with meditation, personal prayer, or in a Quaker Meeting. I am not temperamentally suited to the excited religious stimulation of big gatherings. I find my life is focused in various ways by the experiences of being 'still and cool'. I am aware of being more deeply changed during my twenty years in Quaker Meetings than I was in the previous forty years participating in and leading Anglican worship. It may be something to do with growing older. I am inclined to think that it is the focus on experiences in silence and stillness rather than formal liturgical worship, which has made such a considerable difference for me.

Being thankful

There are so many aspects of life that we accept as normal, without stopping to consider how remarkable they are. For me these include a wide range from the wonders of nature to the essentials of ordinary everyday life: my family and friends, clean water, good drains, my spectacles, an income, a home with its comforts and much more. I could sail along through life simply accepting these as normal for me, taking them all for granted. To challenge myself not to take them for granted, I stop from time to time to appreciate them and many other aspects of life which are important to me.

I find that gratitude only becomes real to me when I articulate it, either to myself or to someone else or when someone else expresses it to me. Either I thank someone for being helpful or kind or I stop and take stock of the multitude of things in my life for which I am deeply grateful. I think by doing so, I nurture in myself more than I otherwise would an aptitude for being grateful. According to *Wikipedia*, research studies show gratitude to be related to personal well-being. Psychologists have only begun to study it in recent years.

Awe and wonder

Another exercise in deep stillness that I value, is to renew my sense of awe and wonder and appreciation of the natural world. Jesus encouraged his hearers not to fret and worry about too many things but find in an appreciation of plant and animal life a unity with creation.[19] We miss a considerable 'wow' factor when we fail to notice the detail of the scent, texture and form of a rose for example, or the wonder and potential of a new-born creature. Articulating to myself my feelings of awe and wonder are important for me. They are further ways into the silence which Quaker *Advices & Queries* encourages us to do. Such explorations allow me to deepen my awareness of the divine and to find an inner source of strength. As the poet W.H. Davies wrote:

"What is this life if full of care, we have no time to stand and stare?" [20]

I also am in awe and wonder as I recognise the unstinting service some people give to others in need during periods of danger, hunger, drought, homelessness, sickness or any other difficult circumstance. Some people are loving and self-sacrificing in serving others in ways that to me are outstanding. Where love shines, I find awe and wonder. I think it important to take time in stillness to recognise it.

Taking stock

The philosopher Socrates in Athens many centuries before Jesus is reported to have said, "The unexamined life is not worth living." I have found it valuable to take time to examine many aspects of my life, reflect on my behaviour and choices, and consider what I need to change. It is very easy to evaluate and criticise the motives and actions of other people: it can be far more demanding to take stock of my own.

As I mentioned before, Jesus challenged hyper-critical people with a verbal quip that reminds me of a Gerard Scarfe cartoon: "Why do you see the speck that is in your brother's eye, but do not notice the log that is in your own eye?".[21] This gives me an image of the nit-picker intensely occupied in trying to remove a tiny speck from someone else's eye, but he cannot do so because he has a great plank sticking out of his own! He can see others' faults but fails to see his own.

Yes indeed, the unexamined life is not worth living. I was brought up short one day, having in my own mind the thought that certain people ought to take a phrase in *Quaker Advices & Queries 17* to heart. Suddenly and surprisingly, the penny dropped for me too. It seemed very much to need to be applied to myself: *Think it possible that you may be mistaken.*[22] I was chastened. I reflected carefully upon it.

In examining myself, I apply some of the lessons I bring from my experience as a counsellor. While I certainly do think it is important to be self-critical, my years steeped in the classic Christian theology of original sin, confession and negativity have given me an impetus to look for the positives too.

If I have done or said something well, I seek to learn from that experience, to see how I can nurture that behaviour or thought. I might wish I had done some things better and will look to see what they might be and how I might do that. If I am pleased with how things went, I reflect on that too and sometimes draw insights for the future.

If on reflection, I feel I have not behaved well, I challenge myself. I aim to reduce the chances of that happening again. I also try take on board other people's reactions or comments and apologise when I feel that is needed. My motto for self-examination is: amplify the positives; diminish the negatives.

I have found it important and helpful to develop my own system of personal review. I make a point of reflecting regularly on *Advices & Queries* which I have treasured for more than 50 years, long before I joined the Society of Friends. However I do regret that in *Quaker faith & practice*, chapter 21 Knowing and Accepting Ourselves, the first few sections 21.07-14 still carry the heavy negative emphasis of classic Christian pre-occupation with personal sin and moral weakness. I have not found that Friends today are much pre-occupied with sin. We tend to be much more positive about human nature in general, while still recognising the awful impact that cruel, selfish or harmful behaviour, or neglect, may have on others.

I like the quotation from Margaret Gibbins who encourages us to share with a friend or Friend some aspects of our life:

"But if two individuals share at an even deeper level from out of their own experience in their search for ultimate reality in life, then the divine in the human shines through and a new creation is born for both." [23]

I recognise the value in sharing with another and finding new insights, encouragement and learning from doing so.

Concerns

For me it was coming to realise 'asking prayer' or 'intercessions' no longer seemed meaningful, that led me to saying 'Goodbye' to God. However, I still recognise the importance of articulating concerns for the well-being of people I care about, for our world and for those who make important decisions on our behalf. It helps me to be clearer in my mind about what I think needs to be done. I prefer now to take time to look as carefully and as thoroughly as I can at any situation and consider what steps seem to be needed to amend, improve, protect or otherwise act.

I might consider: should I take some action? Should I speak to someone about it? Should I write to my Member of Parliament or to a newspaper? Should I join an action group, phone someone, or seek to engage others to join me in taking action? I might feel it appropriate to give some money, or to change my buying pattern by choosing to buy certain things and not others, or change from one supplier to another. I might decide to investigate the situation further and find a book or research something on-line.

On the other hand, I might feel that though the issue is a weighty one, there is little or nothing I personally can do about it. So I grieve for the bereaved, feel for those persecuted or in pain and rejoice with those who rejoice. I adapt the words of the American theologian, Reinhold

Niebuhr, and I "seek the serenity to accept the things I cannot change, the courage to change the things I can, and the wisdom to know the difference".

In the prayer Jesus taught his disciples, the 'Our Father', he longs for God's will to be done on earth as it is in heaven. As a well-known dictum has it, God has 'no hands but ours'. As well as putting thoughts into action, I do feel that what Quakers call 'Holding in the Light' is also an important part of 'soul-silence'. This is to think lovingly and prayerfully about someone who needs help or support. I have a hunch that this can in some mysterious way reach out to them. Am I kidding myself? Am I still attached to what was once important to me? I don't know – I just do it and it feels appropriate. These different activities seem to me ways in which I can respond to Jesus of Nazareth, in a Quaker way, today.

CHAPTER 3

SOME ELEMENTS OF THE QUAKER WAY

We often talk among Friends of the Quaker Way as though what that means is obvious, but 'that ain't necessarily so'. We can easily identify with the atmosphere and feeling of being part of the Quaker community and for many of us that is safe, friendly, supportive, largely respectful of difference, peaceable and active in our local community and further afield. We value the gathering on Sunday morning or at other times, to share in a meeting in which the characteristic is silence, interspersed from time to time by spoken ministry.

Our ethos is such that Friends who share common experiences can be free to account for them differently. As in our business meetings – or Meetings for Worship for Business – we gather to consider specific actions: this is a process of deciding what is right and appropriate, which we call 'discernment'. We make these decisions in a disciplined way, seeking to 'discern' as we are 'led'. We begin in silent waiting, and then listen carefully to views expressed. We often listen further in silence, reflecting on what we have heard, to appreciate the experience, wisdom, or creativity of what has been said or has prompted us to fresh thoughts.

The process by which we come to a decision –

discernment – is that of considering whatever may have been our original thoughts in the light of those shared by others. The Clerk of the meeting has the responsibility to listen to be clear about what she or he thinks is 'the mind of the meeting' and then writes and offers to the meeting a draft minute which she or he trusts truly reflects the mind of the meeting. Only when the meeting as a whole feels that minute, as finally drafted after considering possible amendments, is acceptable, and truly reflects the mind of the meeting, is it accepted.

Sometimes the experience of discernment can take us all by surprise. What seemed so clearly the way to proceed at the beginning of a meeting, may fade as different suggested ways forward seem to be more appropriate in the light of new information. This process is helped by considering the experiences, advice or insights shared during the meeting. These often lead to creative thoughts. It is truly lovely when the meeting comes to a common mind, when those present are confident that a right decision has been reached.

This traditional Quaker way of making decisions, Friends trusted was listening to the promptings of God. As our *Advices & Queries* puts it: *Take heed, dear Friends, to the promptings of love and truth in our hearts. Trust them as the leadings of God whose Light shows us our darkness and brings us to new life.*[1] While Britain Yearly Meeting, our decision-making body, has recorded that wording as our agreed explanation for such experiences, Friends are also at liberty to trust them as loving and rational choices. Many Friends today consider such experiences are natural rather than supernatural or mystical ones. So what one Friend will regard as divine inspiration – the leadings of God – another may regard as a prompting of love and truth that comes from within themselves or from the shared experience and wisdom of Friends in the meeting. We all trust the experience, without being obliged to agree a rationale for it.

Changes in the Quaker way

The Quaker way in Britain has changed over the nearly four centuries of our existence as a religious community. The early Friends were zealous in sharing their message. They had found a wonderful relief from the oppressive doctrines common among Christians of their day. Instead of the fear of God's judgement sentencing them to eternal torment in hell, they were confident that as George Fox dictated in his Journal, "the Lord did gently lead me along, and did let me see his love, which was endless and eternal."[2]

We read about the experiences and thought forms of the 17th century whose culture was very different from our own today. Early Friends were people of their own time; they spoke and wrote of God very naturally. For many people God was a fearsome being, a judge who condemned sins great and small while also being a father who loved and cherished his people. The pervasive culture of thought in those days was of heaven above the clouds. It was envisaged as a life of beauty, glory, peace and joy, presided over by God with Jesus and the angels, saints and loved ones departed, gathered there too. Life on earth below could be tough, unfair, dangerous and for many often oppressive. Further below was hell with its flames to provide eternal torment. Such ideas are very different from those prevailing in our own culture today.

In the 17th century, some preachers, influenced by the teachings of John Calvin in Geneva and John Knox in Scotland, taught a grim gospel of predestination. God had decided from the time each person was born whether they were to go eventually to heaven or hell. Fear and insecurity about life beyond death was a common experience.

However in George Fox's teenage years there was a great ferment of different ideas. These could be widely shared because control of publications by the government eroded during the Civil War. People found they had a new freedom to write and speak about their opinions. They could encourage others to new ideas of Christian practice and teaching. Fox assimilated those from among the radical wing of the English Puritan movement, and those from continental Europe. What emerged in his mind was a synthesis of such thinking, illumined by significant quotations from the bible. The unique aspects of the Quaker way for him was to reject the outward forms and ceremonies of religion with which he had grown up and focus on an inward spiritual reality. His own inward transformation was an experience that he believed was available to anyone who sought it. Two of the Old Testament prophets gave him key elements on which to build his teaching.

The prophet Jeremiah told his people that God promised them a new covenant in which they will not need to rely upon teachers for their knowledge of God for, "Within them I shall plant my Law, writing upon their hearts. Then I shall be their God and they will be my people. There will be no further need for everyone to teach neighbour or brother, saying 'Learn to know Yahweh' (God). No, they will all know me, from the least to the greatest."[3]

This confirmed for George his own experience. A passage from the prophet Joel gave him confidence to share his insights and encourage others to speak of theirs. Joel said that God promised, "I will pour my Spirit on all humanity. Your sons and your daughters shall prophesy, your young people shall see visions, your old people shall dream dreams." This quotation was used by the apostle Peter in his address to the crowds on the day of Pentecost recorded in the Acts of the Apostles.[4]

Fox invited his hearers to attend to their Inward Teacher (Jesus) for he taught that "The Lord would come to teach his people himself".[5] Much to the chagrin of establishment figures, he took the biblical quotations from Joel that Peter quoted as authority for women as well as men to preach. His focus was upon a direct experience of the divine, something that was living and vital in each person who attended to their Inward Teacher. It led to real change in their trust, their values and their behaviour. It had to be expressed in the way they lived their lives.

They felt empowered and confident that God was speaking through them. They felt the urge to share their message widely. As time moved on, this charismatic and prophetic practice gradually changed from the early days of Quaker evangelisation and of persecution, to a quieter period in which the subjective experience of a direct union with God pervaded the Quaker movement.

It was still something to be expressed in the way they lived their lives. They supported one another within their own communities. They practiced a concern for the well-being of the wider community and maintained a personal discipline of integrity under the watchful eye of Elders of the Society. They witnessed to peaceable ways. In time they became pro-active for social concerns to end slavery, to improve living and working conditions for their employees and others. Their community bonded together in inter-family relationships. A Quaker who married a non-Quaker would lose their Membership. Quakers became better at losing members than gaining them until the end of the 19th century when they had a big rethink prompted by a great conference at Manchester in 1895.[6]

In the last 50 years or so, many Quakers in Britain have gradually paid less attention to the bible, to Jesus and to God-language. The Quaker way these days is shaped by the encouragement and challenges offered to us in our little red booklet of *Advices & Queries*. I first encountered it in 1958 and it has changed twice since then.

The language used has traditional concepts of divine leading and guidance which many Friends treasure but others feel do not reflect their current experiences. This creates something of a tension in some meetings and indeed within some individuals. Our key principle is that we have a common way of doing things – gathering in silence, listening to those who are moved to speak, supporting one another in our Meetings, learning and exploring together. Our shared life of meetings and fellowship provides motivation, challenge and encouragement to engage in service to the wider community. The origin of our vision and practice is the teaching of Jesus, as Fox and others first responded to it, and as Friends over the centuries have come to understand and practice its key elements.

For me, the best short description of the Quaker way today is contained in Rex Ambler's book, *The Quaker Way – a rediscovery*.[7] It is a way of:

- **Seeking truth**: the experience of the Inward Light and the light of reason. We are challenged to look carefully at ourselves in the light of Jesus.
- **Looking for God**: searching in the shared silence for a new self-awareness. Waiting in the light to connect with something deep: where it originates from is a mystery but we know it changes us.

- **Meeting others**: belonging to a group which nurtures and serves one another and others beyond that group.
- **Making decisions together**: trusting that the challenge and support of others leads to greater insight, understanding and wiser choices within our meeting and in our lives outside the meeting.
- **Living faithfully**: with a focus on simplicity, integrity, and love, drawing on inner resources which emerge from our trust in silent waiting for clearness, is at the heart of the Quaker way – which is by no means always easy, or without challenges.
- **Bearing witness**: to live authentically to our Quaker Testimony to equality, simplicity, honesty, peace, justice and sustainability and offering an invitation to others to try the Quaker way.
- **Changing things**: if, as a result of our listening in shared silences, we begin to see and feel things more clearly and to listen more carefully to others, we hope to act with them to try to make life better for us all.

What can we now say?

In Britain, church-going and Christian teaching and worship in schools, have declined considerably in the last seventy years. The life of Jesus and other biblical material do not feature in anything like the degree to which they did in the years immediately after World War II. Immigration has also changed the religious landscape of

Britain. Other faith traditions now feature prominently and a secular viewpoint largely prevails here.

The picture is very different in other parts of the world. A report in The Guardian newspaper in August 2018[8] using data gathered in 2015, shows that 84% of the global population identifies with a religious group. About 1.2 billion people, 16% of the world's population, say they have no religious affiliation.

While religion is waning in western Europe, North America, Australia and New Zealand, it is growing everywhere else. As the median age of the world's population is 28, and people of faith have larger families than those who don't practise a faith, the demographic trend is towards people for whom religious practice is important.

There are considerable consequences from this. Religious teachings and loyalties have shaped and nurtured cultures, communities and the mindset of millions. This has benefits in that millions of people are encouraged by the teachings of their faith to engage in social action to help those in need. Many of them campaign to protect the marginalised, campaign for justice and against war, persecution and torture, and have a concern for safeguarding the environment.

Sadly the opposite can also be true: religious convictions can shape opinions to deny justice to others, to promote war and torture, and to adamantly deny that climate change is due to human behaviour. Differences of religion have contributed to wars as we see currently in the persecution of Rohingya Muslims in Myanmar, the Boko Haram insurgency in Nigeria, and fighting between Christians and Muslims in the Central African Republic. There are examples of persecution between followers of different groups within one religion. The divisions in Northern Ireland between Catholics and Protestants remain strong, as do those between Sunni and Shia Muslims in many countries. In the name of religion some sections of society are persecuted: these include women in many cultures, enslaved individuals and families, lesbian, gay, bisexual and transgender people and those who make public their disagreement with the majority religious or political beliefs of the ruling power in the community in which they live.

A current concern in our Religious Society of Friends in Britain from 2019 onwards is to develop a greater empathy and understanding in our own awareness of diversity. We are challenged to look afresh at our organisational culture where "limiting assumptions about race, racism and marginality that may have been unconsciously tolerated in the past will be tackled."[9] A Toolkit for Action entitled *Owning power & privilege*[10] has been produced by Quakers in Britain. Its purpose is to help each of us become aware of the unseen chains that bind us and determine how we live our lives as we explore "Who we are; How we live; and What impact we have".

We are being challenged to recognise that historically

accumulated white privilege is something most of us have grown up with. We have not seriously considered how our basic assumptions interfere with our declared intention to celebrate, value, and promote diversity, privilege and social justice.

Nim Njuguna, in an article in a recent issue of the Friends Quarterly, writes:

"It is now widely accepted among racial justice practitioners that racism in one form or another affects the lives of all people living in a society in which it exists. This is a welcome change from previous approaches that tended to focus on racism as only affecting black people. However, when white people acknowledge that racism is happening, they still predominantly tend to see it in terms of isolated individual incidents rather that the constant grind experienced by most ethnic minority people."[11]

Something similar has been the experience of a wide range of people who are members of other minorities. These include people whose opportunities are limited in our culture by conscious or unconscious attitudes by the healthy, wealthy, well-educated people towards others, who have physical and/or mental illness, are poor, homelessness, or whose sexual orientation, dress or behaviour is challenging or uncomfortable to us. It also must include those many individuals whose lives have been damaged by sexual, physical, or emotional abuse, whether in childhood or in adult life. The contribution of religious people and their mindsets have sadly contributed considerably to their suffering.

Another concern raised by a number of people these days is that too many of us in the secular west are illiterate in matters of religion. We really don't know much about other people's beliefs and practice and we are not necessarily very clear about our own.

Quakers who work alongside members of churches, in Food Banks, with refugees and in other forms of social service in their locality, can find some people are curious about what is distinctive about our Quaker way and values. Have we the confidence to share with them what motivates us and what we find fulfilling in being Quaker?

If we are asked about our religious belief and practice, what are we able to say? If we are asked about our beliefs, or challenged about what is distinctive in the Christian tradition about the Quaker way, what have we to say? The challenge that George Fox made to the congregation in Ulverston church that moved Margaret Fell – "What canst thou say?"[12] is surely still a challenge to Quakers today. If we are clear about the essentials of this way, and of our understanding of Jesus, the gospels and some of the other biblical material, we can help other people realise how positive is a Quaker way of thinking, believing, and living.

Unlike members of some churches, we are not required to subscribe to or recite the Christian creeds. These creeds, which stem from the theological debates of the fourth century of the Common Era, are part of the complex doctrinal statements of classical Christian theology such as the incarnation, the atonement and the Trinity. Church members may be required to recite one or other of the creeds regularly but these statements of belief are not necessarily what motivates their day-to-day life.

Many church members sit lightly to these creeds and few understand them thoroughly. Indeed some acknowledge that they decline to say or sing words of creeds, hymns, prayers and liturgies they feel do not reflect their own beliefs. The atmosphere, fellowship and rituals of the churches have a much stronger attraction to so many people than do the doctrines. The key commitment of most church members is more likely to be to the person and teaching of Jesus as they find him in the gospels, together with the fellowship and spiritual practices of those who seek to follow him.

When Friends who have the confidence to describe our experience of our largely silent worship and Quaker approaches to scripture, to God and to Jesus, many folk are often intrigued. They may be interested to know more. They may find some of our approaches to the way of Jesus has great appeal to them. They may not have really considered that there might be different ways of being Christian, and that particular elements of a Quaker approach might feed their needs in ways which some church practices do not. Some people choose to be both practicing church members whilst also sharing the Quaker way and practice, either informally or in dual membership. Hopefully those who do, get the best of both traditions.

CHAPTER 4
A QUAKER APPROACH TO THE BIBLE

Different religious communities regard their sacred scriptures in a variety of ways. Muslims view the Quran as dictated to Mohammed by God's angel Gabriel. It must be accepted at face value, though it can be interpreted to draw out meanings that may not have been seen before to relate to issues of modern life. Jews revere their scriptures, and delight to explore the many meanings which they can draw from its words.

For followers of Jesus the picture is not quite so clear. There are some who read the gospels almost as Muslims do their scriptures, as if the words were all dictated by God. Many pick and choose which parts they take more notice of than others. Some, while acknowledging the variety of elements in the four gospel books, nevertheless tend to view their content as largely factual accounts of Jesus life. A smaller number have some understanding of the elements of fact, myth, parable, and propaganda which they contain. Stories like the Good Samaritan[1] and the Prodigal Son[2] are so vividly written, some people may be inclined to think they are factual rather than fictional.

Often people's engagement with the bible is with short prescribed passages read in most Anglican, Catholic and Methodist and some other churches on Sundays.

Such short passages of the set readings can distort our understanding of their context unless this is explained at the time. If people are helped to understand there may be deeper layers of meaning in a passage because of the context in which it appears, this can be enlightening for them.

Biblical scholars take into account the social and cultural background of the various writers of the different books of the Old and New Testaments. They seek to set their understanding of what is written within that setting. They draw on modern research methods and knowledge of the historical and cultural context in which the books were written, to illuminate their understanding of their texts. Sadly, this knowledge and these insights are rarely conveyed in church sermons. Many Quakers remain unaware of them too.

There are notable voices of international reputation who challenge the traditional and conservative Christian views, offering a different modern perspective on Jesus, his teaching and his place in history, taking full account of the range of knowledge which we have gained in the last two hundred years. This new knowledge changes our whole perspective on the traditional Christian story and seems to me to be very much of value to the Quaker way. In Appendix 1 at the end of this book I offer some references to the writings of these authors for those who wish to know more.

Jews, Christians and Muslims are known as 'The People of The Book'. We all identify with a tradition that traces its origins to Abraham, the father of the Jewish nation. All three religions respect and value the Hebrew prophets who emphasised the priority of ethical values and behaviour over ritual, peace over war, and social justice over oppression.

The prophet Amos exhorted his people to "seek good and not evil... let justice flow like water, and uprightness like a never-failing stream."[3] The prophet Isaiah had a similar message: "Learn to do good, search for justice, discipline the violent, be just to the orphan, plead for the widow."[4]

The Hebrew prophets echoed the social concerns which earlier generations had enshrined in their Torah or teaching. That promised there would never be poor among them if only they would be faithful to what God required. If any of their people became poor, "Do not harden your heart or close your hand against that poor brother of yours, but be open handed with him and lend him enough for his needs."[5] "You will not harbour hatred for your brother... You will not exact vengeance on, or bear any sort of grudge against the members of your race, but you will love your neighbour as yourself."[6]

Quakers share the biblical narrative with other Christians, and we value the scriptures without taking everything in them at face value. We pay attention to the spirit who gave the scriptures, rather than abiding by the letter of them. Our approach to the scriptures is distinctive, and not widely known or understood, even among Quakers. **To do so, I encourage readers to digest and reflect carefully on the quotations in *Quaker faith & practice* chapter 27. 27-34.**[7]

We find modern knowledge of how the scriptures came to be written helpful in our understanding of how we treat them. The bible contains a number of different types of literature. Some are evidence of historical events, others are literary devices, imaginative creations, poetry, parables, and the Jewish practice of midrash which comments on biblical material and uses it creatively. As Karen Armstrong in her book *The Bible - the biography* explains in her chapter on midrash, the Jewish practice is to look:

"for fresh meaning. In their view, there is no single authoritative reading of scripture… Indeed, a text that could not be radically reinterpreted to meet the needs of the day was dead; the written words of scripture had to be revitalized by constant exegesis…. Midrash was not a purely intellectual pursuit and study was never an end in itself: it had to inspire practical action in the world… and make it speak to the condition of every single member of the community… You did not understand a text until you had found a way of putting it into practice…. Above all, midrash must be guided by the principle of compassion." [8]

We can learn much from the Jewish practice of finding the scriptures a source for creative thinking, rather than regarding them as either a theological straight-jacket or as a consistently accurate historical record.

In the aftermath of the destruction of Jerusalem and its Temple by the Roman army in 70 CE the rabbis ensured the survival of Judaism through transmitting their traditions and their learning in writing. They had intense discussions of their traditions, adapting them to changing circumstances. These they have gathered together in commentaries and interpretations of the Torah.

The Christian approach has had a different emphasis. The three great creeds of the faith – The Apostles' Creed, the Nicean Creed, and the Creed of St. Athanasius which are all to be found in the Anglican Book of Common Prayer, preserve a 4th century understanding of the divine experience and the life of Jesus.[9] However, they say nothing about his teaching, they only encapsulate Christian dogmas. They remain the standard tests of Christian teaching, recited weekly in many church services. Yet the world has moved on, and in the last three hundred years there has been an explosion of knowledge about every aspect of life on this planet and well beyond, of which Jesus, the gospel writers and the framers of the creeds knew nothing.

These days, with so much access to knowledge, research and ideas, we find it difficult to understand how closed was the thinking of people in Western Europe because of the influence of those creeds. Charles Freeman's book *The Closing of the Western Mind*[10] explores the influence they had in inhibiting the exploration of new knowledge and thinking for more than a thousand years.

The Quaker Testimony

The early Quakers did not adopt the creeds. They delved into the scriptures and drew from them inspiration to shape their lives in the circumstances of their own time. This we can do in our day. Our Quaker testimony to truth and to integrity, to equality and justice, to peace, to simplicity and sustainability, all spring from gospel principles which Jesus taught. What was revolutionary in his day may now seem self-evident to many of us, yet all elements of our Quaker testimony are being challenged by current trends in politics, economics and social values.

Truth and integrity are both being freshly challenged by false news, distorted claims, misleading advertising and commercial offers. From the international media we daily hear blatant untruths asserted by presidents, government agencies, and media outlets, as well as by many other people. We discover, only from certain media investigations, whistle blowers, leaks and research discoveries, how officials have made certain statements, which have later been shown not to be true. The testimony to truth and integrity is badly needed as a fresh campaign for the integrity of our common life.

Equality of opportunity and appropriate payment for equal work, respect for difference, and equal respect and treatment is disguised and distorted in many ways in all cultures. Women's voices are now being raised with fresh anger, conviction and power to challenge the injustices visited upon them by a male-dominated power structure. Justice is so often at the mercy of the rich and powerful when legal advice and advocacy are beyond the reach of all but the very rich, or those backed by institutions. The Quaker commitment to equality and justice is an important part of our statements of what it means to follow the Quaker way.

So many countries spend far more on armaments and armies than on building peace, sharing resources, and ensuring peoples' true safety and security in national and international commitments and structures. There are far more sophisticated ways of killing people nowadays than there were in the past. Furthermore, nations and communities can be at the mercy of malevolent powers through the internet and modern technical gadgetry without a shot being fired. The Quaker witness to non-violent protest, and to working for peace and reconciliation between nations, communities and individuals is as important as it ever was.

Our world is being destroyed by the life-styles of the rich and powerful, including our own. We are endangering the chances of sustaining a food supply, lifestyle, fulfilment and well-being for future generations. Apathy about the effects of our life-styles with plastics, waste, fossil fuels, denuded forests, polluted rivers and seas and the loss of wildlife and insects is a grave concern. We work with others to raise people's awareness of our responsibility to the sustainability of our planet.

Quakers in Britain are also currently being challenged to recognise our own power and privilege. In a booklet called 'Toolkit for Action', Suki Ferguson, Quaker Peace & Social Witness Communications Officer writes that our Quaker faith invites us to:

"speak truth to power and challenge those who treat people badly... Unless we challenge ourselves, we risk replicating injustice by default. That's because some inequalities have become normal – we've adapted to them, making them hard to 'see'. And yet inequality is a human problem with human solutions. To make equality a reality, we must choose different ways of being... Discussions of power and privilege often touch upon inequalities that divide us, at a personal as well as a social level. This includes differences in class, income, education, race and ethnic identity, gender, sexuality, age, the spectrum of disability, and personal wellbeing."[11]

The Quaker way has always been concerned about the social implications of our vision of the quality of life and love, as individuals, in families, in our local communities, and in the wider world. The political implications of our understanding of Jesus' vision for people, and our actions to implement them, arise from our silent reflection in our Meetings.

The bible as a source-book

It is important that we have confidence in a creative modern approach to material in the bible. The stories, the challenge to our values and life-style, the presentation of profound wisdom and encouragement to loving actions and service which it contains are valuable source materials for articulating what is enduring about the vision of the early Quakers. It is not a betrayal of Jesus and his teaching, but a fresh appreciation, in the context of our current knowledge, of his vision and challenge to us all. Our world is different from his, and from that of our early Quaker founders and with it the perspective that makes sense to us is different.

Commentators down the centuries, from the earliest days of Christianity, have dealt with the bible in creative ways. Martin Luther King in his "I have a dream" speech did so. So have many great Christian preachers and teachers. It is a recent phenomenon of the last two centuries which has narrowed an approach to biblical material into a literalist view that regards the bible as incapable of being wrong.

Translations into English can sometimes hide nuances of the richness of ideas and meaning in Jesus' parables, poetry and teaching. He spoke in Aramaic yet the gospels were written in Greek, from which we get our English translations. It can be helpful to delve into some of the insights with which specialists in Aramaic language and culture provide us to enrich our understanding of what Jesus was seeking to convey. Doing so can give us a far deeper appreciation of what he meant for example in the Beatitudes (The Blessings), which open the Sermon on the Mount.[12] The familiar translations of these are all too brief and do not convey fully the rich depth of the cultural concepts that lie behind them.

Many people are inclined to think that what we have in the four gospels of the New Testament are first-hand impressions of Jesus, and direct quotations from his teaching. What in fact we do have are selected impressions made on those who heard him, and those to whom they related these impressions, passed on by word of mouth over a period of thirty or more years, and then written down. These impressions were shared in the early Christian communities. They developed and changed over the years of the first century of the Common Era. The earliest gospel, Mark, is short. Later gospels add material of which Mark either didn't know or did not regard as important.

The gospels were then written as creative presentations directed to different groups. Each gospel, while containing much common material, uniquely presents to its target audience the Jesus who speaks most powerfully to them. As one modern commentator writes, he had "a great posthumous marketing team".[13] Each gospel is a literary creation designed to convey to others the impressions that the Jesus story made on his followers. As it was shared with their children and grandchildren, and with new converts, the accounts developed over time. What we have now is 'Jesus remembered' by his earliest followers and learned from them by later ones.

Just as the gospel writers and biblical editors selected those stories and features which spoke most to them, we too can select from the scriptures, narratives which speak to us of love, of grace, of care, forgiveness and service, without getting caught up too much in the pastoral and theological issues or mindset of previous generations. Religious ideas evolve in a variety of ways, as the needs and concerns of people change. We can trace the development of ideas and practices in both the Old and New Testaments.

We also trace such changes in the history of the Jesus movement. In the Middle Ages in Europe there was for a time a great flowering of settled monastic life. This was followed by the emergence of the friars who travelled from place to place preaching and ministering to the wider populace. At the same period, wealthy people invested vast sums to create chantries for priests to pray for their souls. Then came the Reformation and the Catholic Counter-Reformation with profound implications for the life of Christian people. Later in England came the Methodist Movement. This was followed by the great missionary enterprises of the 19th century. Our pre-occupations these days are different from those of previous generations, and we will find in the gospels, a source of inspiration, encouragement and challenge to the issues we face today.

Traditionally the focus has been on Jesus the Christ figure – the divine person. These days many people find it is the pre-Easter Jesus of Nazareth, his life, his relationships, his teachings, and his personality which draws them to review their own lives and values, and seek to follow in some way in his footsteps.

Our Quaker way shares a common narrative with other Christians, and with Quakers worldwide. We need to explore this narrative in ways that are realistic in terms of modern knowledge, offer a credible and enriching spiritual practice, and can creatively help us address many current issues. This gives us a narrative and practice we can confidently invite others to share and explore with us.

Such a narrative, sourced from the gospels, is focused on truth and integrity, community fellowship, trust and service, health and well-being. It values every individual. It has concerns for justice, peace, and for our environment. It is good news to inspire, motivate and change us. It will draw creatively on the Christian tradition, but finds little sustenance in the words of too many classic hymns, liturgies and doctrines.

Its base is a spiritual foundation exploring a variety

of ways of relating imaginatively to Jesus, his life and teaching. It values prayerful silence and leadings in our tradition. It enables us to explore loving relationships, gratefulness, wonder, awe, self-examination (in the spirit of *Advices & Queries*), and service to others.

It may draw on the wisdom of religious teachers from other traditions, but principally draws strength from a creative engagement with the Jesus of the gospels. This will change and develop each of us in our journey to find greater depth, meaning, and loving in our lives. It is important that we share our journey stories with each other, as this will equip us to share such a refreshing narrative with more confidence with people we reach out to and invite them to consider our vision of Jesus' teaching with us.

What was the 'Good News'?

The word 'Gospel' means 'Good News'. Jesus, when challenged to sum up the heart of his message, replied that it is to love God with all our being, and to love our neighbour as we love ourselves. He also quoted the Golden Rule, common to most religious traditions world-wide, and originally it seems to have been drafted by the Chinese teacher Confucius "Do to others what you want them to do to you".[14] It can also be expressed as a negative: "Don't do to others what you would not want them to do to you."

Love is the central theme of Jesus' teaching: this is echoed in passages in other parts of the New Testament such as:

Romans chapter 12: "Let love be genuine. Hate what is evil; stick to what is good. Be affectionate to one another with fraternal love, outdoing one another in showing honour, not holding back in enthusiasm, being ardent in spirit, serving the Lord, rejoicing in hope, steadfast under trial, persevering in prayer, sharing the needs of the saints, cultivating hospitality." ("the needs of the saints" means caring for fellow Christians.)

First Corinthians chapter 13: "…Love is patient; love is kind; love is not jealous; love is not boastful, or puffed up or rude; it does nor insist on its rights, it does not take offence, it does not plan evil, it does not rejoice at wrongdoing but rejoices in the truth…"

Galatians 5.22: "…the fruit of the Spirit is love, joy, peace, patience, kindness, goodness, faith, gentleness, and self-control."

Colossians 3:12-15: "…clothe yourselves in heartfelt compassion, in generosity and humility, gentleness and patience. Bear with one another; forgive one another if anyone has a complaint against another. Just as the Lord has forgiven you, so must you do the same. Over all these, put on love, the bond of perfection."

First letter of John 4. 7-8: "My dear friends, let us love one another, since love is from God and everyone who loves is a child of God and knows God. No one who fails to love knows God, because God is love."

A vision for radical change

We need to bear in mind that Jesus' teaching was no soft option. It took considerable courage, determination, conviction, confidence and creativity to approach life in a spirit of love and non-violent resistance when your homeland is occupied by a cruel and oppressive foreign power.

About sixty years before Jesus' birth, a Roman army had conquered the country and imposed tight political control and heavy taxation. At the time of Jesus' birth, the Jewish King Herod reigned throughout Palestine. He was allowed by Rome a good deal of independence as the local ruler. He died in year 4 of the Common Era (CE) and his kingdom was then divided into three, with his sons as titular rulers. In Galilee, the most northerly province, the local ruler was his son Herod Antipas for the rest of Jesus' life.

A number of groups of men organised armed resistance to the rule of Rome and its subject kings. There was in the tense political atmosphere of that time a keen longing and expectation that soon the long-promised Messiah would be sent from God to set his chosen people free.

One of the charismatic radical preachers in Jesus' lifetime was John – known as the Baptiser. He called people to change their lives, and mark that change by a washing to symbolically cleanse themselves from their old ways, by a complete immersion (baptism) in the River Jordan. John called for people to be loyal to the ethical demands of their Jewish religion.[15] He criticised Herod Antipas for divorcing his wife and then marrying his sister-in-law. Herod imprisoned John to shut him up, and later had him executed.[16]

According to Mark's gospel, after John the Baptist was arrested, Jesus began his mission in Galilee (the most northerly part of Palestine and furthest away from the capital, Jerusalem) saying that then was a critical time – "The time is fulfilled, and the kingdom of God has drawn near. Repent, and believe in the gospel".[17]

Those of us to whom these words are familiar can be under the impression that that sentence is an accurate, complete and literal translation into English of what Jesus said nearly 2,000 years ago. They may or they may not be. They may be Mark's summary of what Jesus was remembered as having said. Furthermore, if we do some detective work on those words, we find there is much more behind each part of the sentence.

"The time is fulfilled" – popular feelings at this time expected the imminent arrival of the Messiah. Many people suggested Jesus was the Messiah but he refused to acknowledge that he thought he was. He more usually referred to himself as "The son of man", a cultural phrase of the time to convey "a man like any other". It features prominently in the Old Testament in two books Ezekiel and Daniel. The prophet Ezekiel used it ninety times as an indirect reference to himself. Jesus seems to identify himself with Ezekiel.

In the book of Daniel, there is a vision of one "like a son of man" or "like a human being" "coming with clouds of heaven".[18] He is given authority to rule over all nations and peoples, in a kingdom that will last for ever. In the gospels, the term 'son of man' is used eighty times. No one else ever refers to Jesus as "son of man". It is always used by Jesus about himself. The claims about his divine status appear not to have come from Jesus himself during his lifetime but from his followers after it.

"The kingdom of God has drawn near" – the Jewish people longed not just for their freedom from foreign oppression, but also for a state where God ruled, where justice and mercy, truth and goodness, prevailed. Jesus was proclaiming that it was soon to happen.

"Repent" – tends to many of us to convey something like regret for what we have done wrong, something we might apologise for. The Greek word in the gospel is *metanoia* which means something like "turn around, and walk in a different direction". He was calling for a radical change in people's values and behaviour.

"Believe in the gospel" – the word translated 'believe' has many nuances in the original Greek. It comes from a common source that includes *to persuade, to seek to convince, to influence*, and many others; all of which really amount to a radical change of behaviour. It is quite different from the common use today of the word 'believe' which is be convinced of an abstract concept, for example in 'to believe thirty impossible things before breakfast'!

So Jesus opened his teaching campaign with a call, following on from John's message, for people to have a revolutionary change of values and behaviour, and be loyal to the vision of God's chosen people, just, true, faithful, caring and compassionate. This was the message of the Hebrew law and prophets.

I see this as still a radical call today, well exemplified in Quaker values and what is known as 'The Quaker Way'. *Bring the whole of your life under the ordering of the spirit of Christ… Remember that Christianity is not a notion but a way.*[19] 'Notion' is a set of ideas: 'a way' is the practical application in life of Jesus' teaching. The message of Jesus' parables and other teaching needs to be internalised and become an essential element of our thinking and behaviour.

Often in Quaker tradition this is known as 'transformation'. It is not a call to believe those thirty impossible things before breakfast. It can be seen as a call to each of us to shape our thoughts, our behaviour, our concerns, ambitions and practice to be as just and as true as possible. It challenges us to have a spiritual under-girding and to be engaged with the values, personality, and teachings of Jesus.

A classic collection of sayings of Jesus is gathered together in what is known as his 'Sermon on the Mount'. In contrast to the creeds of Christianity, the Sermon on the Mount says nothing at all about belief: it is all about how we live and behave to one another. It is contained in Matthew's gospel, chapters 5-7. It is important to realise that Jesus did not speak these words as a complete sermon on one occasion. They are a collection of his well-known sayings, no doubt repeated often in different settings by Jesus and collected together as a key statement of the good news he proclaimed.

The Sermon on the Mount – Matthew's gospel chapters 5 - 7

The Sermon on the Mount begins with what are known as The Beatitudes, or Blessings. These are all about attitudes of mind. Jesus is blessing those who yearn to live justly, those who are merciful, pure in heart, are peacemakers, people who are meek, mourners, and those content with their life as well as those who endure persecution for being faithful to Jesus' teaching.

He compares his followers to salt, which flavours the food it is mixed with, but if it loses its taste, it is useless.

Similarly he compares us to a light, which is not intended to be hidden, but to give light to everyone in the house. Elsewhere, he compares those who follow his teaching to yeast in the dough: even a small amount of yeast can make a big difference to the dough mix![20]

He calls people to follow the teaching of the Torah and of the prophets and by implication to be faithful to the spirit of those teachings not just the letter of them. He reminds his followers that the Ten Commandments state: "You shall not murder". Jesus goes further; he warns them not to allow anger to overrule their judgement. Make peace with a brother or sister, be reconciled to them, and so seek to live in harmony with him or her. He quotes the Ten Commandments: "You shall not commit adultery" but Jesus goes further and says, "Anyone who looks to a woman lustfully has already committed adultery with her in his heart." He counselled against divorce in his concern to foster loving relationships.

In words that George Fox and early Quakers took to heart, Jesus comments on the guidance of the ancients against breaking an oath. He urged his followers not to swear oaths and simply be plainly truthful with "yes" or "no". He quoted a common saying "an eye for an eye, and a tooth for a tooth" which was a way of saying retaliate in kind, proportionately, but not by increasing the degree of retaliation. Jesus encourages his hearers to respond with constructive passive resistance. He went further and asked them to "love your enemies and pray for those who persecute you". He also said if we love those who love us, that is something everyone does. He encourages a more adventurous response from us towards those who are unkind and even persecute us: respond with patience, endurance and love.

He then encourages his hearers not to parade their principled behaviour before others. Don't give ostentatiously to charity or make a feature of praying so that other people see what you are doing. He wants us to do all these things privately, discretely and in simple words. When fasting, make it seem as if you are cheerful and acting normally; keep your self-discipline hidden rather than try to show off about it. He encourages a spirit of forgiveness: just as we hope to be forgiven when we need to be, we must be ready to forgive others when they fail. Recalling the earlier image of light and the lamp, he encourages folk to nurture light within themselves rather than darkness.

Material things he says can be stolen or can deteriorate, but his teaching implies that attitudes, principles, loving actions are where our focus should be. Either our priority is the values of God or those concerned with material goods. He says you cannot serve both equally. In a lovely scenario depicting the world of flowers, birds, and the rest of the natural world, he encouraged his hearers not to fret and worry about material things, but instead strive to love and to encourage others to be loving.

He encourages people not to be judgemental, but to

earnestly seek the riches of a spiritual life that flourishes in loving actions. He then quotes the Golden Rule: "always treat others as you would like them to treat you". Walk a straight path, beware of false prophets, and remember that any fruit tree is judged by the quality of its fruit. So too, his followers will be recognised by the quality of the love they show: "you will know them by their fruits".

Finally, he says that those who not only hear his words but actually act on them, will be like a sensible person who builds their house on a foundation of rock. Storms, rain and tempests will not destroy it. A foolish person who fails to act on Jesus' words and builds their house on a foundation of sand will find it swept away in the wind and the floods.

Quakers are encouraged to remember that our Society is rooted in Christianity and has always found inspiration in the life and teaching of Jesus. We are challenged with "*How does Jesus speak to you today?*"[21] I am seeking to respond to this question for myself: I hope this may be helpful to others.

CHAPTER 5
THE JESUS BOOKS

*Remember the importance of the bible, the writings of
Friends and all writings which reveal the ways of God.
Advices & Queries No 5*

The bible has profoundly shaped our civilisation and
culture, but is not widely read these days, even among
many church members or Quakers. George Fox had
an encyclopaedic knowledge of it and a very retentive
memory. I love the account in his Journal[1] of how Fox
refused to remove his hat in the court in Launceston,
Cornwall where Judge John Glynne, the Lord Chief
Justice of England was presiding. Fox and friends kept
their hats on in court. Glynne ordered them to remove
their hats. Glynne regarded this as a gross discourtesy
and it infuriated him. Fox asked him where in the bible
any king or judge commanded men brought to court to
remove their hats. The judge countered by demanding,
"Come, where had they hats from Moses to Daniel?
Come answer me, I have you fast now," he said. Quick
as a flash, George was able to quote chapter and verse in
the book of Daniel. When three Jews refused to worship a
golden statue erected by King Nebuchadnezzar, they were
sentenced to be thrown into a blazing furnace: "They were

then bound in their cloaks, trousers, headgear and other garments, and thrown into the burning fiery furnace."[2] That is the modern translation. The one Fox used has the word 'hats' instead of 'headgear'.

Fox, it seems, spoke about the Old and New Testaments in some detail in his famous sermon on Firbank Fell in 1652 which really kicked off the Quaker movement. He quoted the prophets of the Old Testament, then the teaching of Jesus, and then the New Testament letters. He also did that in his account in the beginning of the chapter in his Journal dealing with the year 1655. These passages from his Journal show his breadth of knowledge of the whole bible.

The Hebrew scriptures, known to Christians as the Old Testament, are a collection of books of history and ancient stories handed down over many generations. They tell the stories of the foundation of the Jewish nation and the giving of the Law, or Torah, by God to Moses. They tell the stories of the kings of Israel. They also record the sayings of the prophets, the men who interpreted God's will to his people. The story of the creation of the bible is well told in *The Bible – the biography*, by Karen Armstrong.[3]

The books of the Old Testament include poetry, songs, parables and propaganda, together with material recording the visions and declarations of wise men, prophets, and priests. Most of this material was gathered and edited following the great disasters of the occupation of Israel in the 6th century BCE after leading men and their families from the nation were taken into captivity in Babylon. Seventy years later, those who wished to were allowed to return by decrees of the Persian Emperor Cyrus who had conquered the Babylonian empire. They were able to rebuild the Temple in Jerusalem (520 – 515 BCE). The people then concentrated upon treasuring their religious traditions.[4]

As some of the nation's leaders resettled in the Promised Land, literature was produced that was concerned more with the life of the individual, than of the nation as a whole. Known as the Wisdom literature it includes the books Proverbs, Job, Ecclesiastes, the Song of Songs, Wisdom, and some of the Psalms. Wisdom was personified as female. The content is chiefly concerned with proper behaviour in daily life and the individual's relationship with God. True wisdom was seen as godliness.

The nation of Israel was on key Middle Eastern trade routes. It benefited from the creativity which was nourished by the interchange of peoples and their ideas. This Wisdom literature was influenced by writings from neighbouring cultures. The religious ideas and teachings from Confucius in China, the Zoroastrians in Persia, the teachings of the Buddha and the literature of the Hindu communities in the Indian sub-continent, as well as the literature of Egypt and the Middle East, together with the books of the Hebrew Prophets, all contributed to a rich flowering of thought which permeated the thinking of those who wrote the Wisdom literature.

I suggest the finest flowering of this Jewish Wisdom tradition is in the four New Testament gospels describing the life and teaching of Jesus of Nazareth. There are other gospels, often fragments of long-lost books. Many of them contain accounts of Jesus' sayings and actions, some of which clearly are entirely fanciful. These include the Gospel of Thomas, the Infancy Gospels with their fantastic stories of Jesus before the age of 12 using his divine power to do mostly destructive acts, the Gospels of Mary, of Philip, of the Hebrews, and many more.[5] A search of the web for 'apocryphal gospels' will give you a taste of them.[6] The Christian church in the early centuries of the Common Era largely discounted all but the four gospel books they included in their collection which became the New Testament.

Exploring the character and personality of Jesus, and engaging with the key themes of his teaching, can be as fascinating a journey of discovery as any detective novel. In the last two centuries, various scholars have attempted to get behind the gospel accounts in an effort to discover the historical Jesus. Archaeological discoveries in the West Bank area of the occupied territories of Palestine since the 1967 war have brought forward much new information. This, combined with biblical and Jewish studies, with comparative literature and a greater knowledge of the social history of the period, has helped to increase our understanding of Jesus and the era in which he lived.

However, in the end, we simply have to accept that what we really know about Jesus we have from the impressions he made on his earliest followers as recorded in these four gospels. They developed in different ways in the four centres of early Christian life which produced them. It is clear that the authors must have had communication with each other because of the direct copying in Matthew and Luke of most of Mark, and the passages in Matthew and Luke which they have in common but are not in Mark. These three gospels are known as the synoptic gospels because they include many of the same stories, sometimes copied word for word, and generally in a similar sequence.

There are various theories about how the gospels came to be written and for whom. Some scholars suggest the synoptic gospels were written as a course of instruction for new converts. A different view is that Christians wanted to preserve the memory of Jesus for folk who never knew him in life. Another theory is that the first three gospels were composed as a series of readings to complement the traditional weekly readings in synagogues of the books of the Jewish scriptures. Such readings nurtured the first followers of Jesus, who were Jews. They trusted that he was the long-promised Messiah.

Later, the Christian communities became completely separate from their Jewish roots in the synagogues after the destruction of the Temple and city of Jerusalem by the Romans in year 70 of the Common Era (CE). Some scholars today believe that when this happened, the non-Jewish converts to Christianity did not understand many of the Jewish traditions which are threaded through the gospels. That led them to develop ideas of the divinity of Jesus, which Jesus himself did not hold. People throughout the Roman empire were very ready to designate significant people as gods, especially their emperors. What is remarkable is that the titles accorded to the Emperor Augustus 'Lord', 'Son of God',[7] were accorded by the Christian community to Jesus, a peasant from a remote region of the empire.

Whatever the original purposes of the gospels, they were shaped by the traditions and stories of the Christian communities in which they were composed. The personal names they now bear were attributed to them many years after they were in circulation in the early Christian Church, so we do not know who the authors were. Paying careful attention to what modern knowledge can show us about the style, composition and purpose of each of the gospels can help us discover a rich seam of insight, inspiration, challenge and encouragement from Jesus.

While modern scholars can delve into the social, political, and theological threads they find underlying the gospels, most people know little of this, nor of their different explanations for the content and purpose of the gospels. We tend to relate to the text as we find it. That is how these texts have been used for centuries: understood, interpreted and applied to the current situation in every era.

I suggest that while some people will find it enlightening (or confusing) to delve deeper into understanding the gospels, many of us find that becoming more familiar with the text itself gives us material for reflection. This helps us to find inspiration, encouragement, challenge and motivation to seek to live and love in ways inspired by Jesus.

There are many layers and insights which can help us make sense of these four books in various ways. None of them is a contemporary journal of Jesus' life. The earliest, Mark, is dated to about 40 years after his crucifixion. The last to be written, John, is dated close to another 30 years after that. We can trace through the sequence in which they appear to have been written – Mark, Matthew, Luke and John – a story that develops as time goes by. As the early Christian communities reflected on their information, they gradually reframed it. New material was added to the shortest and earliest account in Mark, and the later material in some cases either repeats that in the first gospel, or expands and changes the perception of Jesus. Each builds on the experiences of the community in which they were written.

What follows is just a brief flavour of some things to look for when you read the gospels. I think people appreciate best the style and pattern of each by reading several chapters at one go, rather than just one chapter at a time. All the chapters are short.

Mark's gospel

I began my working life as a newspaper reporter, and Mark's gospel reads to my mind in some ways like a popular tabloid newspaper such as the Daily Mirror. It is a series of articles, mostly very short and vivid, written in the plain everyday language most people spoke. The arrangement is not random: each section has a relationship to others close-by. The author has a structure and artistry in his composition. Some stories are grouped together – parable pages, a healings page, and another with Jesus being challenged by his opponents with tricky questions to answer. An early tradition is that Mark faithfully reported what Peter, the principal apostle, taught, but scholars these days tend to conclude from detailed examination of the text that it developed within a community tradition.

The gospel appears to have been written perhaps in the late 60s, during the four-year war by Jewish resistance fighters against the Roman occupying power. This war culminated in the complete destruction of the city and Temple of Jerusalem in 70 CE, the expulsion of most of the population, and the end of a Jewish state until 1947. It was a time of enormous physical and psychological suffering for the people of Israel. It was also a time of severe persecution of Christians in Rome by the Emperor Nero.[8]

Some of the incidents described have underlying

messages which we miss if we read them at face value. An example is when Jesus turns the money-changers out of the Temple and upends their tables. This is set between two parts of the story of the fig tree that had no fruit on it, although it was not the time of year for it to bear fruit! This is a parable to indicate that the Temple was corrupt, fruitless![9] We need to understand something of the mindset of those who wrote these gospels to grasp fully what they were seeking to convey. A simple literal reading often does not do them justice.

Mark records that two of Jesus' disciples had previously asked him for positions close to him on either side. Soon after we find the closest positions to Jesus on either side are two crucified felons! Beware what you ask for may be the message.[10] The author often positions stories about Jesus to be symbolic. Another example is when the disciples repeatedly fail to realise who Jesus is, Mark puts in the story of the blind man who is healed, followed by Peter being no longer blind to who Jesus was![11]

In many places Mark has traces of the original Aramaic of Jesus. These are stories that will have been told and retold amongst the earliest followers of Jesus, often in response to questions raised by them about appropriate behaviour for a Jew trying to follow the new teaching. "Should we fast? What is OK to eat? Did Jesus expect us to be persecuted?"

In chapter 5 there is the story of Jesus meeting a man who was mentally ill. In those days his illness was described as being possessed by an evil spirit. He lived in a cemetery, was naked, and restrained by chains, but was so strong he broke his chains. He begged Jesus not to torture him further. Jesus asked him his name, he replied, "Legion" because many demons had entered him. The Roman army was organised in legions! Was this a coded message to followers of Jesus during the time of the war that though they were suffering greatly at the hands of Rome, by being faithful to Jesus, his Spirit would overcome even the cruel power of the empire?[12]

Mark is the only one of the four gospels to describe itself as a gospel. It opens with "The beginning of the gospel about Jesus the Messiah, Son of God".[13] This is a carefully chosen echo of the language of the Roman imperial cult of the Emperor Caesar Augustus – "the birthday of the god Augustus was the beginning for the world of the good news".[14] Mark is challenging the imperial myth by deliberately echoing the language associated with the doctrine of the divine Emperor which described Augustus as "saviour" (Latin – *soter*). He presents Jesus, in contrast, as the true Son of God who brings good news to a troubled world. We have become accustomed to such titles being given to Jesus but at the time Mark was writing it would have been an offence punishable by death to suggest anyone was a rival to the Roman emperor. Mark put a number of coded messages in his gospel, to provide protection to both the writer and the readers. He picks up this theme again at the end of his gospel when Jesus is mocked as "The King of the Jews". This was a subversive document in the time of the Roman empire.

Mark begins with John the Baptist's preaching campaign during which Jesus came to be baptised. John was an ascetic preacher, who, though he lived in wild places, drew crowds to his preaching and baptisms. He forcefully condemned common social abuses and exploitations practised in his day by soldiers, tax collectors, and others. He challenged people to make a radical change in their behaviour. He offered them each a fresh start in life, inviting them to submit to a vivid symbolic washing and cleansing of their lives by being baptised by him in the River Jordan.[15] We know of John's preaching and baptising not just from the gospels but also from the Jewish historian Josephus.[16] John had quite an impact in his time: he spoke truth to power, for which he was executed by Herod.

The focus of this gospel is Jesus and his message. The first nine chapters are set in rural Galilee. Jesus, having chosen 12 disciples, moves around with them from village to village, teaching and healing. He spoke in parables: fictional stories designed to catch the imagination of his hearers and remain in their memory. He drew on rural examples, the farmer sowing seed in his fields[17], a lamp lit at night-time[18], and the tiny mustard seed that grows into a large plant.[19] Galilee was then and is now a fertile area where farming thrives with olives, grapes, corn, fruits and vegetables.

He healed a number of people: at least 13 individuals in

chapters 1-10 are named and reference is made to many more. Mark records they were followed by crowds of people from the Mediterranean coastal region of Tyre and Sidon in the north west and from Jerusalem and Judea in the far south, a spread of about 150 miles. Jesus and his disciples crossed the Sea of Galilee, an inland lake, to an area probably about 40 miles from the shore to a place where there were pigs.[20] The distance is estimated because Jews would not keep pigs so this was a Gentile area. Other places mentioned in his journeys in chapters 1-7 include Capernaum, the town on the edge of the Sea of a Galilee, his home village of Nazareth, and the village of Bethsaida nearby, before he moved further afield to the coastal region of Tyre and Sidon, a distance of about 50 miles.

In Mark's gospel, Jesus is depicted as "the hidden Messiah", recognised eventually by his followers as such, but always wanting to avoid public adulation as he goes about teaching his revolutionary way of living. From chapter 10 he moves towards Jerusalem, 85 miles to the south, down the valley of the river Jordan via the ancient town of Jericho. All the while he is teaching in parables, healing, meeting people, reacting to the crowds and those who came pressing questions on him. It is a lively and busy sequence of events. He was interacting with people all the time.

Mark allocates most space to his vivid account of the last week of Jesus' life. Chapters 11-16 presents Jesus' entry into Jerusalem on the Sunday before his crucifixion on the Friday. He goes into the Temple area and physically throws out the sellers and the money-changers trading there.[21] He seeks to emphasise it as a place of holiness, not a place to fleece the faithful. This act appears to have been the principle reason for his arrest later in the week and his eventual death. At a time of high tension for the Passover festival, when crowds of pilgrims would have travelled from near and far, the High Priest and his council wanted to keep the peace in the city. It is clear that Jesus alone was regarded as a threat to peace, for none of his disciples were arrested and tried with him.

In chapter 13 he forecasts the destruction of the Temple and the city, with great suffering: events which duly happened when the Roman army eventually destroyed the city and the Temple. This description may have been written after the event, but presented as a prophetic statement.

The action then moves rapidly to his preparation to leave his disciples. He shared with them a last meal in chapter 14, before his arrest, trial, torture and crucifixion. During this trial his chosen friend Peter becomes frightened of being identified as a supporter of Jesus and denies he has anything to do with him. Jesus is deserted by the other male disciples as well. After his death, his body is taken down from the cross, and buried in a nearby tomb lent by a wealthy sympathetic supporter.[22] This gospel ends with Jesus' death and burial, and the women who came after the sabbath and found the tomb empty. Years later someone added verses 9-20 to provide an account of the resurrection, presumably by Christians concerned at the lack of this important element.[23] That, however, was not part of the earliest version of this gospel.

Mark's gospel seems to have been written to convince those in the Roman world that in spite of his rejection by the religious authorities of his time he was truly the son of God whose life and death and resurrection are of benefit to humankind. It is a message to hold fast in a time of persecution and remain faithful, come what may, to the person of Jesus and his message. It was also written with the expectation that Jesus would return within a short period of time. Then God's kingdom on earth would begin: a society in which the love, the justice, the care which Jesus taught and exemplified would reign supreme. The Christian community was focused on preserving certain particular kinds of memories of Jesus: those that would persuade other people of his special status and significance and to discover for themselves the implications of discipleship. This exerted a strong selective influence on what this gospel contains.

Matthew's gospel

If Mark reminds me in style and composition of a tabloid newspaper, Matthew reminds me of the Daily Telegraph in that it has much more content than Mark, and is conservative in its approach. It features Jewish traditions and quotes extensively from the Hebrew scriptures.

The religion inspired by the life and teaching of Jesus grew first in Jewish communities. This was a time when there were various Jewish groups, some with strong convictions, reform movements or mystical unions. One of these groups was the Essene community who are thought to have hidden the Dead Sea Scrolls in sealed earthenware pots in lake-side caves. The Jesus followers, who were first named 'Christians' at Antioch,[24] were just one of many such groups.

The author of the gospel of Matthew was clearly a Jew, well versed in the Hebrew scriptures. He writes to convince other Jews that Jesus was the Messiah because so many references in those scriptures seem to point to him. At the same time he is angry and intemperate in his references to those Jews who would not accept Jesus as the Messiah. He is clearly a leader of one Jewish group concerned to oppose and criticise other Jewish groups. He calls the Pharisees, who were conscientious observers of the Jewish Torah, hypocrites.[25] He blames the people of Jerusalem for the death of Jesus.[26]

Matthew opens with the sequence of Jesus' ancestry[27] beginning with Abraham, whose covenant with God is the foundation of the Jewish nation. Most readers tend to skip over this sequence of names, yet it contains some interesting features. It includes four women who each conceived a son in unusual – we might describe them as 'shady' – circumstances: Tamar[28], Ruth[29], Bathsheba[30], and Mary.[31] It also includes Rahab[32] who was a prostitute who helped Joshua's invading army to capture the city of Jericho. Jesus' ancestry is traced through Joseph, though Mary is described as a virgin! I wonder what the editor of this collection was aiming to communicate to those who heard his words, by this genealogy. I also wonder why he included these five women, three of whom (Tamar, Rahab and Ruth) were not Jewish.

He goes on to give an account of the visit of wise men from the east, followed by King Herod's attempt to kill Jesus by ordering the slaughter of all baby boys under two years of age. To avoid this, Matthew tells us that Mary, Joseph and Jesus escaped to Egypt.[33] There is no independent historical verification for the events so described. The account strongly conveys parallels to the life of Moses who was a survivor from Pharaoh's edict to slaughter all Jewish baby boys. He brought the Jewish people out of their enslavement in Egypt.[34]

Matthew's account is a creative way of declaring that Jesus is a second Moses: more significant than Moses who was the source of Jewish law and traditions. This literary device is characteristic of the Jewish cultural practice of building on the familiar and significant episodes in the lives of Jewish patriarchs and prophets. Episodes in the lives of Abraham, Moses, Samuel, and Elijah are re-presented in the lives of subsequent key men, especially in the life of Jesus. The accounts of Jesus' birth in Matthew and Luke are contradictory. Most biblical scholars these days recognise that those birth narratives are not historical.

Matthew features the work of John the Baptist, who called people to confess their sins, change their lives and be baptised in the River Jordan. This was to symbolise a cleansing from their former ways. They rose out of the water to a new clean life. Jesus too came to be baptised by John. There he was acknowledged as the son with whom God was well pleased.[35] Matthew follows this with a description of Jesus' 'temptations in the wilderness'[36] (the psycho-drama as I described it in chapter two). Jesus then chooses as his base for his ministry in Capernaum, a lakeside town in Galilee. Matthew presents this action as fulfilling a prophecy of Isaiah for the Messiah to issue his message in Galilee.[37] Jesus challenges his first four disciples to join him in his mission, and begins work, teaching and healing in Galilee and the Jordan valley.

Unique features of this gospel are five distinct sections of Jesus' teaching material, each of which concludes with "When Jesus had finished these sayings…"[38] Some scholars suggest this pattern is a deliberate midrash application to Jesus' life and ministry of the five books of Moses. These books, known as the Torah (Teaching) are the first five books of the Old Testament: Genesis, Exodus, Leviticus, Numbers, and Deuteronomy. They are the most revered books of the Hebrew scriptures. Matthew clearly identified five sections of his gospel as distinctive teachings. Jews at the time this gospel was written would have understood their significance and their relationship with the Torah.

The first of these sections in Matthew is the Sermon on the Mount[39] which I outlined in some detail in the previous chapter. The second one deals with the choice and mission of his twelve apostles and Jesus' instructions to them to expect to face persecution.[40] The third of these is a teaching section using parables drawn from the agricultural life of the area, the sower, the weeds amongst the wheat, the mustard seed and the yeast. Matthew provides some explanation so that they might be better understood.[41]

The fourth teaching section[42] turns normal thinking upside down in that when he was asked, "Who is the greatest in the kingdom of heaven?" Jesus called a child to him and told his disciples that "unless you change and become like little children you will never enter the kingdom of heaven." Innocence and trust seem to be the characteristics he is extolling. He puts great emphasis on pastoral care as a shepherd cares for his sheep and searches for one lost sheep while ninety nine are safe in the sheepfold.

He also teaches them the importance of forgiveness, teasing Peter who asked how often he should forgive a fellow member of the Jesus community – as many as seven times? Jesus replied, "Not seven, but seventy times seven." I don't think he meant Peter to count to 490 –

but to take his point that a readiness to forgive should be without counting.

His fifth great teaching section is set in Jerusalem, detailing the coming destruction of the city, the need for watchfulness, and the fact that there will be a time of judgement coming for all nations.[43] From there the Jesus story moves on to his betrayal, his last Passover supper with his disciples, his prayer and agony in the garden of Gethsemane, arrest, trial, and then the offer by the Roman Governor Pontius Pilate to release either Barabbas or Jesus. Matthew declares the crowd opted for Barabbas the robber. Jesus is mocked, crucified, dies, and is buried.[44]

Then comes the bombshell: the account of the resurrection of Jesus with the discovery of the empty tomb. Matthew accuses the chief priests of bribing the guards to say someone has stolen the body. Matthew states that the Jews were still telling that story at the time he was writing. Finally, Jesus commissions his disciples to take his teaching to all nations, making disciples everywhere.[45]

Matthew's gospel aims to show Jews in particular, or at least a group of them who were confident that Jesus was the Messiah, that God was at work in and through Jesus. Matthew is convinced that Jesus fulfilled so many elements mentioned in the Old Testament of what God would do in the future. He quotes almost anything he can find to indicate that what those Old Testament passages foretell was fulfilled in the life of Jesus.

None of the gospels are what we might call straightforward biography because each of them sets out to proclaim a message to portray Jesus as the local Christian community believed him to be, the long-promised Messiah, the son of God. In his book *Biblical Literalism – a Gentile heresy*[46] Bishop Spong argues that Matthew's gospel (like those of Mark and Luke) was probably written as complementary readings for use in synagogues where a considerable proportion of the congregation had come to regard Jesus as the long-promised Messiah.

Luke's gospel

The gospel of Luke reminds me of the newspaper I read daily: The Guardian. It has a strong social concern and features the role of women in Jesus' ministry. The writer is clearly interested in health, healing and social justice. It is more cosmopolitan than the other gospels as it is clearly directed not just to Jews but to Gentiles as well. It is the first part of a two-volume book. The second volume is the Acts of the Apostles. The author presents himself as an historian, seeking to address a Roman called Theophilus (the name means 'One who loves God') to ensure that he has a true account of Jesus.[47]

Luke is a good story-teller whose descriptive language, dialogue, scene-setting and memorable characters provide some of the most popularly known and treasured Jesus material. These include the story of his birth at Bethlehem with shepherds, informed by angels, coming to the stable[48] and of Jesus as a boy questioning the wise old men in the Temple.[49] He presents his scenes vividly. In places he uses imagery from the world of business, with debtors, creditors and cheats. A key concern of his is to show that Christianity is not a threat to the Roman empire. He therefore holds the Temple authorities, not the Roman Governor Pontius Pilate, responsible for Jesus' death.

He describes his work not as a 'gospel' as Mark does, but as an 'ordered account', implying that others have fallen short in their work of relating the life and work of Jesus. Some scholars think he has modelled his work on two historians of the era: Dionysius of Halicarnassus who wrote a history of Rome, and Josephus who wrote a history of the Jews. All three authors provide dates for the birth of their respective founders, Romulus, Moses and Jesus, and relate their births to other events around that time. They describe the circumstances of each founder's birth in which both Romulus and Jesus are described as 'sons of God'. Each describe the teachings of their founder. Both Romulus and Jesus appeared to witnesses after death, and ascended to heaven![50]

Luke was written to be read aloud, to Greek-speaking listeners in the Roman world familiar with divine figures such as Roman emperors. The author is seeking to clarify the position of Christians in relation both to the Roman empire and to Judaism. He emphasises that Christians are not a threat to the empire as his kingdom was not of this world. In contrast, although Jesus and his first followers were all Jews, the Jewish leaders have rejected Jesus and caused his death. The Christian mission is now focused on Gentiles.

Luke gives a very different account from Matthew of what happened at the time of Jesus' birth. His story-line begins with the promised birth of John the Baptist and the ante-natal encounter of Jesus' mother Mary with John's mother Elizabeth. This incorporates hymns which were being sung by early Christians: Zechariah's, Mary's, and Simeon's songs which later generations have come to know as the Benedictus, the Magnificat, and the Nunc Dimittis. This is clearly a piece of creative writing.[51]

This gospel takes the holy family from Nazareth about 100 miles south to Bethlehem; Jesus is born in a stable and a heavenly choir of angels sing to shepherds on night duty. There is no mention of wise men, Herod's slaughter of baby boys, or an escape to Egypt. This account is a literary device to convey to readers the great significance of the life of the man who is the central character in this gospel. It is not factual but is seeking to convey a religious insight to understanding the perceived significance of the man who his followers (forty or more years after the crucifixion) by then regarded as divine. Reading back in time it portrays a significance that was not realised at the time of his birth. This is not a deliberate deception, but a literary device not at all unusual in that era. It was used for Augustus Caesar and others. Symbolism is mixed with memory to convey 'this man was extraordinary'.

Luke describes in vivid detail the preaching of John the Baptist. We get a real flavour of John's moral teaching and his ethical demands as well as his tongue-lashing, threatening sinners with hell-fire. "There was a feeling of expectancy among the people," Luke reports. However John's public preaching was too much for King Herod, who clapped him in prison. So, it is suggested, Jesus took over the mantle of John, though it seems in a less fiery manner.[52]

Luke then provides an invented genealogy of Jesus. Whereas Matthew with his genealogy starts at Abraham (the father of the Hebrew nation) and moves forward to Joseph and Mary, Luke works back from Jesus not just to Abraham but beyond him to Adam, the reputed father of all humankind. The message in this gospel is that Jesus is not just for Jews but for everyone. I describe both genealogies as invented because there were simply no such records available to consult and the two versions, whilst having common elements, have significant differences too.[53]

Luke also provides an account of Jesus' temptations – the psychodrama I mentioned in chapter 2. Immediately after that he begins his ministry and as in Mark's gospel, Jesus sets out on his journeys around Galilee, teaching and healing. This time, when Jesus gets to his home village of Nazareth and preaches in the synagogue the congregation turn against him! It seems he was not at all surprised at that. They tried to kill him but he got away safely.[54]

Jesus is portrayed travelling round Galilee, teaching, healing and commissioning his disciples. In chapter 6, Luke includes some of the same material that Matthew has in the Sermon on the Mount, in a section often called 'The Sermon on the Plain'.[55] There are a lot of parables recorded in Luke, a number of which are not included in the other gospels: the Lost Sheep, the Lost Coin, the Prodigal Son, the Unjust Steward (or the Crafty Manager)[56], the Rich Fool[57] , and the barren Fig Tree[58]. It is a great read.

From chapter 19.28 he enters Jerusalem for the final week of his life.[59] He clears out the traders and money-lenders and in a week of increasing tension with the Temple authorities. He teaches, warns, argues and denounces his opponents in the build-up to his betrayal and arrest. He agonises before the arrest, accepting its inevitability yet still pleading in prayer to God "if you are willing, take this cup away from me. Yet not my will by yours be done."[60] This is a poignant moment of both fear and courage. Jesus had previously warned Peter that he would betray him before the cock crowed three times.[61] Peter insisted that was something he would never do. Yet, when Jesus is arrested and taken to the house of the High Priest, Peter, standing outside was accosted as someone who knew Jesus. His courage failed him. Three times he denies knowing Jesus. When the cock crows, Jesus turns and looks at Peter, who promptly goes outside and weeps bitterly.[62]

Jesus is sent to the Roman Governor Pontius Pilate, then to Herod the ruler of Galilee who sends him back to Pilate. From there he goes the 'Way of Sorrows' to Calvary. He is crucified and ridiculed, yet he is able to be compassionate to one of the thieves crucified beside him who asks for his help. Jesus promises him they will be together in paradise. Luke gives us a vivid picture of darkness and death, as Jesus dies, watched by the women who had followed him from Galilee.[63] Luke then tells us that a member of the Jewish Temple council who had not agreed with the others in seeking the death of Jesus asks Pilate for Jesus' body, wraps it in a linen cloth and lays it in a rock-hewn tomb that had never previously been used for anyone else.[64]

Luke's story-telling continues with his account of the women followers coming at dawn with spices for the body. They discover the large stone that sealed the entrance to the tomb has been rolled away and there was no body in the tomb. They encounter "two men in dazzling clothes" who terrify them at first, then reassure them, and tell them to report to Jesus' friends – "but this story of theirs seemed like an idle tale, and they did not believe them." Peter goes to check and comes away from the empty tomb amazed.[65]

Then Luke provides another unique story – two of the disciples, later that day, walking to Emmaus, are joined by a man they do not recognise. The three talked together as they walked and it was only when this person is invited to join them for a meal in a house in that village, that as he blesses and breaks the bread for the meal, they suddenly realise it is Jesus. Then he vanishes.[66] Later he appears to the whole group in Jerusalem, speaks with them, eats some of their fish, and instructs them to wait in Jerusalem until they receive 'power from on high'. The gospel ends with the ascension of Jesus.[67] Luke's account of the growth of the Jesus movement continues in his second volume, the Acts of the Apostles. There he describes the growth of the church and the spread of the Christian message through the Roman world.

John's gospel

John's gospel is different again. As I compare the previous gospels to British newspapers, John reminds me of how I remember The Sunday Times in my youth. It reflected on the week's events, with long carefully researched 'Insight' articles which looked behind the scenes of the current news.

The result is a gospel in which one or more authors, and perhaps one editor brings together different sources, after having clearly spent many years meditating on the person and message of Jesus. A 'portrait' of Jesus is presented, threaded through with profound reflections on who Jesus was. We have long discourses addressed either to his closest followers, or in arguments with religious leaders in Jerusalem, on interpretations of 'what Jesus must have said', whereas the other three gospels portray Jesus mostly speaking to crowds who throng to see and hear him.

The book as a whole has sections which seem detachable; the thread of the book doesn't flow as it does in the other gospels. The famous Prologue in the opening chapter[68], magnificent as it is, seems unconnected with the rest. In chapters 3-7 Jesus moves between Galilee and Jerusalem and some scholars think the order should have chapter 4 in Galilee and Samaria followed by chapter 6 which is also set in Galilee. Chapter 5 would then be followed by chapter 7 – both set in Jerusalem. Many ancient manuscripts do not have chapter 8, verses 2-11 and bibles usually note that these verses seem to have been inserted after the rest of the gospel was compiled.[69]

At the end of chapter 14 Jesus is reported saying to the disciples, "Come now, let us go" – but then his discourses with them continues for the next two chapters! The resurrection appearances in chapters 20 and 21 appear to be unrelated episodes, gathered from different sources, and then joined together. Chapter 20 verses 30 and 31 seem to conclude the gospel; this is then followed by chapter 21 with a second conclusion in verses 24 and 25.

Some scholars think that chapters 2-11 are drawn from another source, which some call the 'Book of Signs'. Turning water into wine is the 'first sign'.[70] Clearing out the traders from the Temple is another sign.[71] These are then followed by others including the healing of the son of a royal official[72], the cure of a man at the pool of

Bethesda[73], the miracle of the feeding of the large crowd[74], Jesus walking on water[75], a man born blind[76], and the raising of Lazarus.[77]

John places the eviction of the Temple traders and money-changers from the Temple courtyard during Jesus' first visit to Jerusalem, at the beginning of his ministry. The other three gospels put this at the end of Jesus' ministry after his entry into Jerusalem on 'Palm Sunday'.

John's gospel portrays Jesus over three years with three visits from his northern homeland to Jerusalem in the south. The other gospels give just one year for Jesus' ministry and just one visit during that ministry to Jerusalem. Mark sets the pattern that Matthew and Luke follow, but without giving a timescale. Many scholars these days regard John as probably having a more historically accurate account of several incidents, particularly the timing of Jesus' trial. This gospel has many other differences from Mark, Matthew, and Luke. In them, Jesus' ministry is mainly in Galilee as he travels to different villages, hillsides and seaside areas. In John the action is mainly in Jerusalem. The style here is very different, with Jesus portrayed as focusing a great deal on himself and who he was: "I am the Good Shepherd"[78], "I am the Light of the World"[79], "I am the Bread of Life"[80], "I am Son of God"[81], "I am the True Vine"[82], "I am the Resurrection and the Life".[83]

Central to the theme of this gospel is the long 'Farewell discourse'[84] in which Jesus prepared his disciples for him leaving them. He is reported to have said, "I give you a new commandment that you love one another, you must love one another just as I have loved you. By this everyone will know that you are my disciples if you have love for one another."[85]

The author, or editor of this gospel, has a deep knowledge of Jewish practices, and of the city of Jerusalem. He draws on material from the Hebrew scriptures which only a Jewish person would have been familiar with. He is compiling a Jewish 'Wisdom' book about Jesus, steeped in the tradition of Jewish mysticism, using metaphors and stories about named people (many with names which are very significant to Jewish traditions) who appear nowhere else in the gospels. Spong in his book *The Fourth Gospel*[86] is convinced these are all literary creations, not historical individuals. They are presented to convey a profound message of the significance of Jesus.

Spong challenges the concept of 'literalism' in trying to make sense of John's gospel. He writes:

"John is not about literalism. His understanding of Jesus is not about what Jesus literally said or what Jesus literally did. John is a Jewish writer, writing a Jewish book that transcends literalism at every point, and he draws his major images from Jewish mysticism, as he seeks to tell the story of Jesus' life as one who transcends limits, breaks barriers and invites us all into a new place that he represents. This gospel is not about God becoming human, about God putting on flesh and masquerading as a human being; it is about the divine appearing in the human and calling the human to a new understanding of what divinity means."

So Spong suggests the miraculous signs which are a prominent feature of this gospel are not to be taken literally, but are creative ways to see "Jesus as the doorway into a new consciousness, which is also a doorway into God, who might be perceived as a universal consciousness." Spong's book on this gospel provides a great deal of helpful insight into making sense of what is otherwise a rather lovely but bewildering account of Jesus. For me this gospel is a far more meaningful source for reflection since reading what Jack Spong writes about it.

The gospel has nothing at all about Jesus' birth and early life. Its account of Jesus' ministry begins in chapter 1.19 with the witness of John the Baptist, who is recorded as describing Jesus as "the lamb of God"; a few verses later the disciple Philip describes Jesus as "he of whom Moses in the Law and the prophets wrote, Jesus, son of Joseph, from Nazareth."[87] These and many other references would be deeply meaningful to first century Jews but puzzling to most Gentiles.

The scene in which Jesus chooses his first disciples is described very differently from the descriptions of it in the other gospels.[88] After this comes the incident at a wedding in Cana in Galilee[89] when Jesus is reported to have changed water into wine, described as the first of the significant 'signs' that he performed.

Then the scene suddenly shifts from Galilee in the north, a hundred miles or so south to Jerusalem for Jesus' first visit there at a Passover when he chased out of the Temple traders and money-changers.[90] Chapter 3 features a long intimate conversation with a Jewish leader Nicodemus. After this Jesus spent some time in the countryside near Jerusalem baptising people (though the author later explains in chapter 4 that it wasn't Jesus who was baptising but his disciples). This is happening while at the same time John the Baptist was still baptising nearby!

Much of chapter 4 is taken up with a long conversation that took place on his walk back to Galilee. He met by chance a Samaritan woman at a well. Another detailed intimate conversation is recorded. After some time in Galilee, presumably a year, he then returned to Jerusalem for another Passover. Here he cured a man at the Pool of Bethesda on a sabbath day, after which Jewish leaders began to persecute him for not properly observing the sabbath. Jesus gives a long reflection on his life and mission.

In chapter 6 we have an account of Jesus feeding 5,000 men, then walking on the stormy surface of the Sea of Galilee, followed by him preaching in Capernaum and reflecting on his feeding miracle with his teaching "I am the bread of life".

A further visit to Jerusalem for the Feast of Tabernacles

is described in chapters 7-10 at which he speaks more of his mission and role. He cures a blind man, and speaks of himself as the good shepherd, and as the son of God.

From chapter 11 he moves towards Jerusalem and his death. The first scene depicts him raising his friend Lazarus four days after death. Jesus declared, "I am the resurrection and life." It is after this that Jewish leaders plan to kill him. There is the touching scene at Bethany, about four miles from Jerusalem, where Mary, the sister of Martha and Lazarus, brought costly scented ointment to rub on Jesus' feet. The next day Jesus rode into Jerusalem on a donkey. This is John's Palm Sunday story, without the eviction of the money-lenders from the Temple. He warned his disciples that he is going there to be killed. He spoke of himself as "the light" and urges his followers to trust in the light "so that you become children of light".[91]

Throughout the gospel there is an air of puzzlement/ scepticism as people who see and hear him ask questions about who he is, and how he is able to do the things he does. "He came to his own and his own people did not accept him."[92] It is thought by many scholars that the drafting of this gospel reflects the developing tension and separation between the Christian community (all Jews at first and then a growing number of Gentiles) and the traditional Jewish community which did not accept Jesus as the Messiah. This separation grew more pronounced after the destruction of Jerusalem in 70 CE; antagonistic references in John's gospel to 'the Jews' should be read as the 'Jewish leaders of the synagogues'. The strong antagonisms in this work sadly contributed much to 2,000 years of anti-semitism.

Chapters 13-17 contain the long farewell conversations of Jesus with his disciples at their last supper together. It begins with his act of washing their feet, a symbolic act of service and cleansing. He comforts and encourages them, all the while apparently aware that Judas was acting to betray him to the Temple authorities. He warns them of the challenges, opposition and persecution they will face as they seek to be faithful to his message. He promises them that the Paraclete – the Holy Spirit – will be with them to strengthen and support them. He envisages returning very soon and prays for them in words of tenderness and intimacy.

The action towards his end begins in chapter 18 where he is arrested in the Garden of Gethsemane at night. He is taken to the High Priest to be questioned. While this interrogation happens, Peter, outside, speaks to someone. His northern accent identifies him as a Galilean. He is challenged and asked if he is a follower of Jesus. John simply records: "Again Peter denied it, and at once a cock crowed."[93]

The High Priest sends Jesus to the Roman Governor Pontius Pilate who, after questioning Jesus, apparently wants to release him. Pilate offers the crowd a choice of releasing Jesus or a robber called Barabbas. The crowd shout for Barabbas. Pilate then famously "washed his hands" of the matter. In chapter 19 Jesus is beaten, condemned to death, and crucified. As he hangs in torture on the cross, he commends his mother into the care of "the disciple whom Jesus loved."[94]

Jesus dies and is buried in a tomb lent by a follower of his, Joseph of Arimathea. Two days later, Mary of Magdala is reported to be the first one to the tomb; she finds it empty. Peter and another disciple follow her, check the empty tomb, and go back home. Mary, standing outside the tomb weeping, encounters someone she at first thinks is a gardener, but suddenly realises she is talking to Jesus. He tells her not to cling to him as he is yet to ascend to his Father.

Later that evening Jesus appears in a closed room to his disciples and breathes on them the Holy Spirit. Thomas, who doubted the story of Jesus' resurrection without having experienced seeing him for himself, finds his doubts dissolve. The final chapter, 21, is an account of Jesus meeting his disciples on the shore of the Sea of Galilee near the town of Tiberias, where they share breakfast. There he forgives Peter his denials in the courtyard. The gospel ends with the writer stating there are many other things that Jesus did.

John's gospel portrays Jesus as very human. He weeps at the death of his friend.[95] On another occasion he is tired and hungry.[96] If you are puzzled by some of the features of this gospel, particularly turning water into wine and raising to life a man who died four days previously, you may find enlightenment in reading Bishop Jack Spong's book *The Fourth Gospel*.[97] His is only one view of course, but it may set you on a journey of discovery in other books too.

Belief then and now

The gospels are products of belief and traditions of 2,000 years ago. Our knowledge and understanding of the world has changed dramatically. Many of us do not understand the events in the same way as those who lived even 200 years ago did. While we can accept that Jesus believed he was given a mission from God, we may or may not accept that explanation for his life and ministry. Some may be able to give a large degree of credence to the gospels, as someone like the scholar Bishop N.T. Wright does. On the other hand, many other scholars view these gospel descriptions from a variety of perspectives. I believe we can find in the gospels much to reflect on: prompts to creative thought, to self-examination, to insights, and aids to look afresh at our values, our relationships, and our behaviour. This is so whether we accept the world-view and theology of Jesus, or not.

A key element of the Quaker way is that we are invited to be true to our own experiences and understanding. Within the Quaker tradition I believe we can still share the journey of those Friends who hold deeply traditional views, for we share many similar experiences even if we describe them or account for them differently.

CHAPTER 6

REVISING OUR UNDERSTANDING OF THE JESUS STORY

Our understanding of Jesus and his role in the history of humankind has to change in the light of modern knowledge. We now know that life on earth emerged and developed in various forms over millions of years. This makes the traditional Christian world-view of creation and redemption long taught in Western European culture, literally unbelievable.

The classic Christian salvation story is rooted in the biblical picture of God creating the world and all living creatures in a state of perfection in the Garden of Eden. Adam and Eve sinned and were ejected from the garden, so God needed to mount a rescue operation. He sent his son Jesus to be a human sacrifice to "die to save us all".

That was a story that could make sense to previous generations who had very limited knowledge of the actual origin of human beings and the world in which we live. As with any other field of knowledge, when information changes, we adjust to that new information: our understanding and our explanation of things changes.

We know that human life did not begin with Adam and Eve but that all life has evolved and continues to evolve. Not only do we share 99.9% of our DNA with other primates like the great apes but we share DNA connections with cabbages and with plankton and so many other living organisms! There was no original perfect couple from whom we are descended, whose sin has tainted us all. Instead, we are in a stage of evolution from primitive origins and we continue to share links with even very basic forms of life.

An element of life common to all species is that we are orientated to survival, and this drives the evolutionary process. It is true of both animals and plants. In humans, the survival urge means we are self-centred. We do not easily relate to people who are different from us. Our self-centredness can show itself in our behaviour and in our prejudices. What previous generations described as an inclination to 'sin', we can recognise as aspects of our human development.

The Christian faith has a long history of emphasis on sin. One of the most negative aspects of this for me, (a former member of the Church of England), is the statement in the confession at the start of Morning and Evening Prayer which is still regularly used in English cathedrals even if it is less used in local churches: "We have followed too much the devices and desires of our own hearts, we have offended against thy holy laws, we have left undone those things which we ought to have done, and we have done those things which we ought not to have done, and there is no health in us."

The idea that we are all so depraved that there is "no

health in us" is to me appalling. As children we all learn to love by being loved, not by being subject to constant criticism. Jesus' teaching again and again is positive about love. At the same time he is critical of behaviours which demonstrate a lack of love. Look at just three examples in the gospels of how Jesus encouraged his hearers to focus positively on love, care and compassion.

There is the lovely fictional story Jesus told of a Jew who travelled alone on an isolated road between Jerusalem and Jericho.[1] He was waylaid by thugs, beaten, robbed, and left half dead by the roadside. In turn, two religious men came along the road, saw the man but "walked by on the other side". Next came a Samaritan, a member of an ethnic group with whom Jews would normally have nothing to do. He saw him, dressed his wounds, lifted him on to his mule or donkey, took him to an inn, and paid for his care while he recovered.

Jesus told that story when challenged by a lawyer to tell him what he must do to "inherit eternal life". Jesus responded by asking him what was written in the Jewish Torah. The lawyer quoted Deuteronomy 6.5 and Leviticus 19.18 which provides the classic summary of the law – to love God and to love your neighbour as yourself. Jesus told him he had answered truly. But the lawyer pressed further, and asked, "Who is my neighbour?" Jesus told him that story and afterwards asked the lawyer, "Who was neighbour to the man who was robbed?" The lawyer couldn't bring himself to say the words "The Samaritan" so instead he said, "The one who showed mercy towards him." Jesus replied, "Go, and do the same yourself."

There is another story that doesn't really belong in John's gospel but has been tucked in there by some later editor[2]. It is the story of a woman "caught in the very act of committing adultery" (for which the law prescribed death by stoning) brought to Jesus by those who opposed him. They were trying to catch him out in order to bring an accusation against him if he disagreed with what the law prescribed. They pressed and pressed him to say what should happen to her. Jesus eventually said to them, "Let the one among you who is without sin be the first to throw a stone at her." Those who intended to trap Jesus into a compromising answer gradually all drifted away. When just Jesus and the woman were left, he said to her, "Has no one condemned you?" When she replied that no one had, he simply encouraged her to go home and change her ways.

Yet another parable – or fictional tale – Jesus told was of the owner of a vineyard who employed casual labour who stood in the market place seeking work. Those he engaged at dawn agreed to work for one denarius for the day. Later in mid-morning, at noon, at mid-afternoon and finally close to sunset, he engaged more and agreed to give them each a fair wage. At the end of the day he paid all his workers the same amount – a full day's pay.

Those who had worked from the earliest time expected more than those engaged near the end of the day, and they grumbled, complaining they had borne the burden and heat of the day. The owner said he was not being unjust to them – they had agreed the pay rate at the start of the day, and he the owner chose to pay the last as much as the first. He was generous, knowing that all of them had the same need to provide for their families. This generous attitude is a hallmark of Jesus' approach to life.[3]

The teaching of Jesus leads us to look afresh at this strong tendency in us to protect ourselves, and to be critical of others. He challenges us to find ways of loving that are more generous, less self-focused, more caring and aware of other people's needs (as well as our own) and adjusting our behaviour to not only care for those closest to us, our parents, siblings, partners, children, and grand-children and so on but to offer generous love to others too. These other people may be very different from us, and we may find it difficult to like or to understand some of them. Any of their unkind, rude or churlish behaviour to us may lead us to close in on ourselves in order to protect ourselves and those closest to us.

Finding a more open and generous way of dealing with these situations, though very demanding of us, leads or can lead we believe, to a better quality of life and relationships for everyone in our community and to benefits in the wider world.

We Quakers are encouraged to: "*Respect the wide diversity among us in our lives and relationships. Refrain from making prejudiced judgements about the life journeys of others. Do you foster the spirit of mutual understanding and forgiveness which our discipleship asks of us? Remember each one of us is unique, precious, a child of God."* [4]

Miracles and myths

Religious traditions tend to have tales of the supernatural – of miracles. What on earth are we to make of them in the context of what we now know about what is normal and what is abnormal? Some Christians take these accounts at face value – historical records of actual happenings. Those of us who cannot accept them in that light, seek to understand the background from which these accounts arose.

We have to begin with the particular cultural mindset of the Hebrew people in Jesus' time which is not that of most people in modern western society. The Jewish midrash tradition features characteristic stories about significant people which were re-presented in later generations to indicate the special significance of certain later individuals. An example is the common story of how three key figures in biblical history were conceived when their mothers had more or less given up expecting to be able to have a child.

The ancient and mythical story of Abraham's wife Sarah who becomes pregnant with the help of divine intervention at the age of ninety[5] and gives birth to Isaac, is re-presented in the conception of the prophet

Samuel. His mother wanted a son and when she promised to dedicate him to God's service in the Temple, lo and behold, she conceived and gave birth to Samuel.[6] The story is re-presented again in Luke's gospel in relation to John the Baptist, son of elderly parents who had long faced the prospect of no children.[7]

An original folk-tale is taken up and re-presented in later generations to declare this particular person as special, in the way the earlier story says someone a long time ago was special. It is a creative fiction to us but was significant to people many centuries ago as it fitted their mindset and knowledge. If we can accept that, instead of trying to demonstrate these things must have happened because God could make them happen, we can read these stories as myths – that is, stories with rich significance and meaning to people in the past that can have a significance for us today. We won't stretch our imaginations to try to reconcile folk-tale with history.

A similar thing happens with the stories associated with both Moses and Elijah which are re-presented in the stories about Jesus in the gospels. One of these concerns the events when Jesus was born, as recorded in Matthew's gospel, which hark back to events at the time Moses was born. According to the account in the book Exodus, the king of Egypt, Pharaoh, was so concerned about the growing population of the Jewish community in Egypt whom he saw as a threat to his people and thus to his rule, that he ordered the midwives to kill all the Jewish baby boys at birth. When Moses was born, his mother hid him for three months. When she could hide him no longer, she placed him in a waterproofed basket and hid him at the riverside among some reeds. His older sister stood at a distance to watch what would happen to him.

Pharaoh's daughter came to the river to bathe, spotted the basket, and discovered its contents. She took pity on the baby and arranged to pay a Hebrew woman (who happened to be his mother) to rear him for her. When the child grew up, his mother took him to Pharaoh's daughter who adopted him.[8] The elements of this story reappear in Matthew's account of Jesus' birth. The Magi arrive from the east, seeking the new king of the Jews. The actual king, Herod, is not amused, but hides his malevolence behind a mask of apparent interest in this new king. When the Magi do not return to Herod to report where they found him, Herod orders the slaughter of all baby boys under the age of two to ensure the destined king has to be included in this slaughter. Meanwhile, Mary, Joseph and Jesus escape to Egypt.[9]

There is no independent historical evidence for either slaughter. The idea that searching astrologers can be guided by a star, like a laser beam, to a stable at Bethlehem is fanciful. However, if the creative mindset of the author of Matthew's gospel is to portray this person as greater than Moses, then we can begin to understand why he wrote into the story of Jesus' birth circumstances which mirror those around that of Moses. Add to this the parallel that Moses came from Egypt to the Promised Land: Jesus and his parents also come from Egypt to the Promised Land when it was safe for them to do so. Here you have a typical Jewish scenario, all to the effect that this Jesus was like Moses only greater than Moses.

These accounts are not historical records but creative fictions to link the story of Jesus with that of Moses and so to boost his significance. It is a cultural tradition. It can strike the modern sceptic as dishonest, but in a culture where people were used to stories being re-presented in this way it was simply a means of proclaiming the significance of Jesus.[10]

Christianity separated from its Jewish roots

We have to remember that the earliest Christian communities were all Jewish. In the catastrophe of the war of 66-70 CE when Jewish groups revolted against Roman rule and the Roman army then defeated the Jewish resistance, the Romans destroyed the city of Jerusalem and its Temple. This was a game changer for the Christian movement. It became separated from its Jewish roots and became increasingly non-Jewish, that is Gentile. That was when these stories began to be regarded by Christians more as factual than part of the Jewish midrash tradition with which they were not familiar.

Moses lived about three hundred years before the stories

about him in the bible were recorded. These stories and the miracles associated with him, are more like folk tales, told and retold, growing new elements as they were passed on down the generations. His life and actions feature in the second book of the bible, Exodus. At the period depicted the Egyptians kept very detailed records of events. There is no hint in them of this biblical saga.

A well-known miracle ludicrously illustrated in the Cecil B DeMille film The Ten Commandments, is the parting of the Red Sea to allow the children of Israel to escape the pursuing Egyptian army as they made their way out of slavery to freedom in the Promised Land. A mistranslation of the Hebrew words which mean Sea of Reeds have been repeatedly translated into English as the Red Sea. This has played havoc with this story, for the Red Sea is two hundred miles wide of deep water and way off the route that Moses and his people would have needed to take to get from Egypt to Palestine.[11]

The area they could have crossed on their route was the Sea of Reeds. It was an area of swampy marshland. The escaping Hebrews – walking, carrying very little – were pursued by Egyptians mounted in heavy horse-drawn chariots. It would be difficult enough for those being chased to cross this area but it was impossible for the charioteers whose vehicles sank into the marshland. As the story was passed on down the generations and sung about in words recorded in Exodus chapter 15, verses 1-19, it developed in the minds of those who heard it as being more like DeMille's version than what actually might have happened.

This story came to be **the** example of God's miraculous power over water – repeated in the story of Joshua and the Hebrew people crossing the river Jordan to enter the Promised Land after the death of Moses.[12] Later stories were told about the prophet Elijah and his successor Elisha and of their power to part the river Jordan in order to cross safely.[13] It is suggested that the gospel stories of Jesus walking on the Sea of Galilee, and of calming a great storm on that sea are really to say that Jesus had powers similar to and greater than Moses had when it came to dealing with water.[14]

Another famous miracle event associated with Moses is the provision of 'manna from heaven' to feed his people as they journeyed through the arid wilderness.[15] Some scholars have suggested the origin of this story is in the white flaky substance that falls from the tamarisk trees in that area, which the people could eat. As the story was related and then recorded and edited it grew into a key story of God feeding his hungry people with 'manna' from heaven.

In all four gospels there are versions of the story of Jesus managing to feed 5,000 or 4,000 people miraculously.[16] Those who struggle to relate the idea of food appearing in this way, can find a different understanding of why the accounts are there in the gospels if they read them in the context of the Jewish midrash tradition. What the gospel writers were really seeking to convey was that Jesus was enabled by God to do what Moses did and to do it even better than Moses could.

Another great figure in Jewish history is Elijah.[17] He was a thorn in the side of King Ahab, and his Queen Jezebel, as he was critical of Jezebel's devotion to the god Baal. Stories about Elijah feature his ability to call on God to create drought, to call down fire from heaven, to provide a poor widow and her son with an unending supply of meal and oil to sustain them in a famine and to raise the son to life after he died. Elijah is the man who, escaping from capture by the queen's men, reached a mountain where he encountered God not in the earthquake, wind or fire but in a "still small voice" as the traditional version has it. In a modern translation this becomes "the sound of sheer silence".[18]

Elijah is called home by God in a dramatic fashion. Accompanied by his under-study Elisha, they journey towards the wilderness for a meeting with God but the river Jordan bars their way. Elijah sweeps his cloak over the river and its waters magically part to allow the two of them to cross on dry land.[19] The parting of the waters achieved by Moses and Joshua is thus repeated, before Elijah dramatically ascends to heaven.

Elisha copies his master Elijah in parting the Jordan with Elijah's cloak, he too raises a child from the dead, later he heals a non-Jew, Naaman the Syrian.[20] Miracles associated with water, with feeding, with healing, with ascending to heaven[21] are all attributed to Jesus. They are regarded as the prerequisite of a notable man of God. Jesus too is reported to have raised the son of a widow from the dead[22] as well as doing so for Lazarus, the brother of his friends Martha and Mary.[23]

I am indebted to Jack Spong for this perspective on the miracle traditions of Hebrew scriptures. He writes:

"Moses, Joshua and now Elijah are said to have power over nature. Moses and Elijah have the power to expand the food supply. Moses, Joshua and Elijah have the power to split a body of water so they can navigate across it on dry land. Elijah adds to this collection of biblical stories the raising from the dead of the only son of a widow. A pattern is clearly developing. Perhaps when we look deeply enough, we will see that they were never intended to be supernatural stories of divine power operating through a human life. Perhaps we have been defending an idea that even the biblical authors never intended."[24]

There are many Christians who are happy to read of such miracles in the gospels as factual records of what Jesus was uniquely able to do. Others of us, who revere Jesus and his remarkable teaching while remaining sceptical about such accounts, find they make more sense to us as literary traditions of an earlier age than as miraculous powers that strike us as impossibilities.

Resurrection!

The resurrection experience of the first disciples is to me a puzzle, as it is to many others. As Maurice Casey states in his *Jesus of Nazareth*:

"The belief that Jesus rose from the dead has been a central feature of Christianity from the earliest times. Scholars have however found the origins of Christian belief in Jesus' resurrection very difficult to understand."

He concludes that "belief that Jesus had risen from the dead was held at a very early date". He goes on to argue that the earliest belief was not based on the empty tomb nor on the stories of resurrection appearances in the four gospels. It rested upon the expectations of the disciples from what Jesus had said to them before his death, and what they made of passages in their scriptures.

He notes that all the resurrection appearances of Jesus were to his followers. No one else experienced them. He explores in some detail the phenomenon of resurrection appearances of recently bereaved people reportedly seeing their loved-one and even speaking with them.

He proposes that the appearances:

"may reasonably be called 'appearances' because that is how those people who saw them interpreted them, and so did the early tradition about them. They may reasonably be called 'visions' because that fits everything we know about them, in a culture in which visions were normal, and considered perfectly real."[25]

Similar experiences are known today. In my ministry as an Anglican priest I heard a number of such visions described by bereaved people which enormously comforted them. I am also aware that groups of people can share visions. It is suggested that group and individual experiences of this kind shaped the development of the resurrection story.

Marcus Borg and J.D. Crossan in their book *The Last Week* state:

"Without Easter, we wouldn't know about Jesus. If his story had ended with his crucifixion, he most likely would have been forgotten... So Easter is utterly central. But what is it? ...So central is the historical factuality of the Easter stories for many Christians that, if they didn't happen this way, the foundation and truth of Christianity disappear. To underline this claim, a verse from Paul is often quoted: 'If Christ has not been raised, then our proclamation has been in vain and your faith has been in vain' (I Corinthians 15.14). We agree with this statement, even as we do not think that it intrinsically points to the historical factuality of an empty tomb."[26]

They too explore in detail the various accounts in the gospels of the resurrection appearances, and whether the records are factual or parables. They believe that those who had such visions of Jesus were convinced that he lived in a radically new way from that of his previous existence before crucifixion and death. For them, Jesus had become a figure of the present, not simply of the past.

That is true too for many Christians today – their experiences in prayer convince them that 'Jesus lives', he hears their prayers, they feel close to him, he is for them companionable, guiding, protecting, and sustaining. Such experiences can indeed be profound. Those who have never encountered such experiences, nor have heard of them first hand from those who have had them, can be deeply sceptical about their reality.

Borg and Crossan say:

"not all visions are hallucinations. They can be disclosures of reality. Moreover, visions can involve not only seeing (apparition) and hearing (audition), but even can have tactile dimensions, as dreams sometimes do. Thus a story in which Jesus invites his followers to touch him, or is seen to eat, does not intrinsically point away from a vision. People who have had a vision report that something important and meaningful, often life-changing, has happened to them – they would never consider trivializing it as 'only a vision'… Paul came to believe Jesus is Lord because his experience of the risen Jesus changed his life".[27]

Geza Vermes, a former Professor of Jewish Studies at Oxford and translator of the Dead Sea Scrolls, examined six theories that have been put forward to explain the resurrection of Jesus and concluded that this resurrection was in the hearts and minds of his followers, not a physical resurrection. He writes:

"Resurrection in the hearts of men may strike a note of empathy even among today's skeptics and cynics. Whether or not they adhere to a formal creed, a good many men and women of the twenty-first century may be moved and inspired by the mesmerizing presence of the teaching and example of the real Jesus alive in their mind."[28]

The pattern of death and resurrection to new life was a crucial element of the early Christian message. Converts were invited to undergo a process of transformation by dying to the old life and rising again to the new one. This was vividly acted out in the practice of baptising converts, after a period of preparation which could last up to a year. The baptisms took place on the eve of Easter Day. People renounced their old life, washed it away symbolically in total immersion baptism, and then began their new life in Christ. Various scholars consider the gospels to have been written principally as courses in instruction and preparation for these converts before their baptism.

A political dimension

Jesus was crucified not so much, it seems, because of his religious teaching but because the High Priest and his Council deemed him a trouble-maker who threatened the peace of the city at a festival. It was the High Priest's responsibility to ensure peace and prevent riots. He did not have the authority to order Jesus' execution, so he handed the problem to Pilate with a recommendation to execute Jesus. Pilate promptly did so.

There is still more to this than most people realise. We read the gospels simply as accounts of Jesus and his ministry. What is not obvious to us is that these Jesus stories were not just about personal religious experiences, there was a political dimension to them. The early Christian movement was subversive to the imperial powers of Rome. '*Jesus is Lord*' was a political statement that Jesus, not the Emperor, was Lord, in the lives of his followers.

Remember, the gospels were written around the time of the war of 66 -74 CE during which the Roman army destroyed Jerusalem and its Temple. Mark chapter 13 is heavy with warning about the coming suffering Rome was about to impose upon Jesus and his followers, when there will be "great distress, unparalleled since the beginning of creation".[29] Luke also has this warning[30], as does Matthew.[31] These convey horrific scenes of death and destruction, imposed by Rome. It may be that they were written after the Jewish experiences of Roman barbarity, but presented in the gospels as examples of Jesus foretelling what was going to happen.

The early Christians believed that Jesus' passion for the kingdom of God, where the God-given values would prevail, stood against the values of the rulers of this world. Borg and Crossan argue that *'Jesus is Lord'*, the most widespread post-Easter affirmation in the New Testament, is thus both personal and political. It involves a deep centring in God, that includes radical trust in God. That was the same trust that we see in Jesus. Its theme is freedom – "For freedom, Christ has set us free; compassion, love and courage 'Fear not, do not be afraid'." They go on to argue that this is the centring in God that empowered and inspired Dietrich Bonhoeffer to work for the overthrow of Hitler, Desmond Tutu to challenge apartheid in South Africa, and Martin Luther King Jr to continue his campaign for civil rights for all Americans in view of all the threats he faced.[32]

Crossan writes of this political opposition to Rome and its values in his book *God & Empire – Jesus against Rome, then and now*.[33] The Christian community resisted the religion, culture and values of the Roman empire. Whereas Rome saw itself as winning peace through military victory and control, the church in contrast worked for peace by peaceful methods of non-violent resistance.

The last book in the New Testament is *The Revelation of John*. It is reported to have been the favourite book of George Fox because it pointed to what was to come, rather than what had been. It is a vision of war in heaven between the Devil and his angels against Michael and his angels. John Milton's powerful poem Paradise Lost is based on this. Revelation is a complex book full of imagery which is not clear on face value. Those who engage with it need to have some understanding of what each of the elements in it is representing, to get its full implications.

The purpose of the book is to reassure Christians who are being persecuted that Christ will triumph over the evils of Rome's imperial rule. Rome is represented as "the whore of Babylon" and "the scarlet woman".[34] Its empire will be superseded by the new heavenly Jerusalem, coming down out of heaven, "dressed as a bride for her husband".[35] Those who remain faithful will share in its life and will triumph over evil, war and oppression.

It was this vision which so sustained the early Quakers who endured around thirty years of intense persecution in the reign of King Charles II and later. From their reading of Revelation they expected persecution, felt it a badge of honour. This vision sustained them while they were imprisoned, beaten, had their property distrained and were hounded out of their Meeting Houses.

New life in Christ is the transforming vision which has fed the hopes of Christians now and in the past. It is not just a religious experience but a social transformation as well. It is a powerful story and it began with those events, however we understand them and explain them, of those early disciples whose lives were transformed by their experience of resurrection.

Healings

There are numerous descriptions in the gospels of Jesus healing: a man with a withered hand[36], two blind men[37], a deaf and dumb man[38], ten lepers[39], even one instance where the crowd was so great the man's friends couldn't get near Jesus so the story is that they removed part of the roof of the house Jesus was speaking in, and lowered their friend down on a stretcher to be healed.[40] There are references to other examples of Jesus' healing: two from blindness, two from leprosy, one each from fever, a haemorrhage, a withered arm, deaf-muteness, paralysis, lameness and dropsy.

Frankly I expect there to be some exaggeration in these accounts, but equally I am sure that Jesus was renowned as a healer. People who have the power of healing, either through prayer or some other medium, are well-known the world over. While many claims are indeed exaggerated, the phenomenon of healing is and was in Jesus' day, often associated with holy individuals. He was not the only well-known healer during his lifetime. Historians of the period describe the work of a man named Honi the Circle-Drawer, or named as Onias the Righteous by the Jewish/Roman historian Josephus. Another healer was a fellow Galilean, Hanina ben Dosa.[41]

Such charismatic people have an intense belief in their being a channel of healing. While the modern sceptic, whose opinion is that healing only happens when modern western medicine is applied, may scoff, I am sure that a number of healing changes have occurred in the lives of people because of the intervention of wise women, shamans, and individuals including some clergy and religious and laypeople who have discovered a power in themselves who have brought about cures for sick people. George Fox was noted for his ability to heal in this way.[42] The culture, social context, relationships, love, and other motivating psychological factors can all have healing influences.

The mind can have a remarkable effect on the body. When I was a hospice chaplain, I often worked with imagery to help people manage their pain, in addition to whatever medical treatment they were receiving. I helped a number of people who were able to work with imagery in this way and to take some personal control of their pain.

Modern medical research uses blind trials in which placebos, with no expected curative powers, are given alongside the actual new medication being tested. In such trials none of the recipients or their doctors are aware of which is which, only those conducting the research know. Curiously an average of about one third of the placebos are effective in making a healing difference in those who take them. When we expect something to do us good, it can do.

A BBC television programme Horizon broadcast on October 4th 2018 entitled *The Placebo Experiment: can my brain cure my body?* featured an experiment carefully designed by medical academics from Oxford University. There were 117 people in Blackpool who suffered from chronic back pain who took part in the experiment, all taking daily doses of a blue and white capsule. They were told that some were taking a placebo, and some a new drug. All were in fact taking a placebo – just under half of them found their experience of pain changed remarkably.

The researchers' technical machinery could demonstrate changes in the brains of these people similar to changes which analgesics can produce. This showed that for those for whom the placebo worked there were physical effects produced in the brain. These reduced or removed their experience of the pain. Some of them had suffered from back pain for many years, which had very much limited their freedom of movement. Even more curious is the fact that when everyone was told they all had been taking placebos, some continued to do so, and continued to feel the benefit they experienced when they thought they might be taking a new medication.

I am not batting for any one of the healings that are attributed to Jesus in the gospels, but I know healings can happen in this way. I imagine this is because the recipient believes it is possible. So I sit lightly to these accounts of Jesus healing – some may be exaggerated, some may be reasonably accurate. He certainly was convinced of his ability to heal people, and taught his disciples to do so too.

CHAPTER 7
SOME QUAKER RESPONSES TO JESUS

The Quaker response to the teaching of Jesus began in the years around 1640-1660 in the life and teaching of George Fox and other early Quakers. That was a time of great ferment of religious ideas both in England and in parts of western Europe. Traditional Catholic teaching was being challenged by a variety of ideas which emerged from the Protestant Reformation.

Leading figures of the Reformation such as Martin Luther in Germany, John Calvin in Geneva, John Knox in Scotland, Ulrich Zwingli in Switzerland, the Dutchman Desiderius Erasmus, and the man who virtually single-handedly wrote the English Book of Common Prayer – Thomas Cranmer, all contributed their ideas to what was required for true loyalty to the teaching of Jesus.

At the same time, England was not well served by many of its parish clergy. Their income came from tithes – a tax of 10% paid by all householders yearly on all their produce and income. It was widely resented, and too many clergymen seemed more concerned about their tithes than the pastoral care of their people. In quite a number of cases, the Rector, the person entitled to receive the tithe, might be a lay person, a landowner, or an Oxbridge college. The Rector would appoint a deputy,

(Latin: *vicarious*) called a Vicar, and paid him a small proportion of the tithe.

While the traditional education for clergy was at the universities of Oxford or Cambridge, the content of this education was more classical Greek and Latin literature, than Christian theology and pastoral practice. Much of what these men taught from pulpits was dry, arid, and uninspiring or else it was full of the fear of hell-fire and damnation. Ordinary people would struggle to find love, joy, peace, and patience in the words of most of the sermons to which they listened.

It was also a time of political ferment. King Charles I was a pious man of rigid convictions. He believed that as king he was God's anointed and had a divine right to rule by personal diktat. He tried to manage without reference to parliament. His intransigence forced people to rebel as they argued for the English tradition of government by king and parliament working co-operatively. The tensions between the royalists who supported the king and the supporters of parliament had developed from the beginning of his reign in 1625 and boiled over into armed conflict in the summer of 1642.

One of the consequences of civil war was that the government was in chaos. Censorship of printed material, which hitherto had been tightly controlled, suddenly relaxed. For the next fifteen or so years there was an upsurge of fresh ideas in circulation largely through popular pamphlets for there were no newspapers in those days. There was a freedom to promote ideas of which the early Quakers made full use.

George Fox

(See note with References at the end of the chapter to a biography of George Fox, and an account of the Quaker story.)

George Fox, born in 1624, was still a teenager in the early 1640s. He was disillusioned with what he was hearing from professional preachers. He spent four or more years searching for a religious teaching and practice that could satisfy his deepest longings. He travelled quite extensively to listen to the professional preachers of the Church of England and to those of the Independent congregations but found no one who could satisfy that for which he was searching. When his quest seemed hopeless, he had an experience in which he heard a voice within him declaring, "There is one, even Jesus Christ, who can speak to thy condition." The impact on him was enormous – he said, "My heart did leap for joy".[1]

His long and lonely search among teachers of the Christian faith culminated in that vivid experience. He read the bible endlessly and digested it thoroughly (he had an excellent memory and could recall scripture at will). He reflected upon all this prayerfully and formed a clear vision that he felt impelled to share with other people. He was convinced that the experience he had was something anyone else could have – if they were open to it.

He believed that he was looking at contemporary life with the mind of Jesus. His message was not narrow nor especially religious. He applied what he learnt of the teachings of Jesus to the issues of his day. He felt he was called to bring people from "their own ways to Christ, the new and living way".[2] This meant they broke the habits of a lifetime, bound by what he referred to as "vain traditions and dishonest ways". They were to reject the paraphernalia of the church rituals which he was convinced were "men's inventions", and be freed from their "windy doctrines" to "the new and living way". His teaching came to many people as a breath of fresh air.

He made a sharp distinction between the inner life of the Spirit, in which anyone could discover God's truth and presence if they sincerely wished to do so and the life of "the creature", the ordinary human society with its corruption, deceit, greed and suffering. Some of his teachings were already circulating in the exchange of ideas that the civil war enabled to be widely shared. What he did that was different was that he was not only deeply critical of the values and practices of his day, but he offered something positive as an alternative.

He called this "turning to the light" – quoting John's gospel[3]: "The true light that gives light to everyone, was coming into the world". The key Quaker doctrine he taught was that the "light" of Christ is in everyone, of whatever religion, race, or culture. What mattered was how anyone responded to this "light". He regarded his insights as a gift from God by which the freshness of the original Christian message was being rediscovered. It fed people inwardly with a vision and power that changed their lives profoundly and would change society too.

George was not a theorist but a practical man. He never defined the "light" but always spoke of what it does in the life of a person. For him it was the active principle of God working in us. His mission was to get people to bring their lives to that light. He used various words to convey the one inner reality of spiritual and moral growth in people who turned to that light. It was like a new birth. For him, lived experience was key.

This was going to involve conflict, for the light showed up the darkness in people's lives and then gave those who turned to it power to overcome the weaknesses and inadequacies of human nature, what was traditionally called sin. It offered people a new understanding of themselves, not as 'miserable sinners' but as human beings with great potential, able to be filled with the indwelling spirit of Jesus. It was not a life in isolation but a life nurtured in the community of others who opened themselves to the light. He and his first followers initially called themselves "Children of Light". In 1650, according to his Journal, Fox urged a judge, Justice Bennett of Derby, to "tremble at the word of God". Bennett retorted by calling them "quakers". They took the name as a badge of honour.[4]

Whereas the church preachers taught that people should look for the second coming of Christ, Quakers preached that Christ had come already: "God was come to teach his people himself..."[5] This was their challenge to the people of England and indeed to the whole world. The conflict that this conviction aroused, Fox described as "the Lamb's war".[6] He drew his imagery from the book of Revelation, the last book of the New Testament – it was a contest of good against evil. Fox and his Friends were committed to passive resistance, fighting hate with love, violence with gentleness, persecution with endurance. He called people to a relationship with Jesus who would rule their hearts, teach them his ways and care for them.

The Quaker impact

The Quaker message when first shared publicly, began to have a big impact in English life. Some of the Quakers we most admire, such as George Fox, Margaret Fell, William Penn, Elizabeth Fry, John Woolman and many others, had such an impact on the people of England in their day that there were echoes of Jesus' challenge to the popular culture and practices of his day in Galilee. Like Jesus, Fox was also a radical thinker and an engaging preacher. He encouraged his followers to have a relationship personally with Jesus in the gospels: to seek insight, guidance, and spiritual strength in a direct approach to God, largely through waiting and listening in stillness and silence.

Fox grew up in his local church where his father was churchwarden but in his teens he rejected the establishment of the professional preachers and church systems. He was deeply critical of their ideas and practices. He refused to pay tithes to the parish clergy whom he described as "hireling preachers". He refused to accept the hierarchical culture of his day with elaborate and rigid distinctions between people of different social classes. He addressed every person with equal regard whether aristocrat, courtier, justice, housewife, tradesman, servant or labourer and in the same direct terms. He spoke plainly to all. He lived simply, and encouraged his followers to do so too. He wanted no double-standards of truth telling, so refused to take any oaths in courts. These actions, and the fact that he welcomed and encouraged female Quakers to preach and share their message, infuriated the establishment of his day.

He was regarded as a dangerous revolutionary and after the restoration of King Charles II in 1660, parliament with bishops in the House of Lords leading the way, took steps to ban Quaker meetings, and severely punish with fines, imprisonments and beatings those Quaker men, women and children, who met in largely silent meetings, or who spoke publicly of their convictions.

Women played a substantial and important part in spreading the Quaker message. Among them was Margaret Fell, a woman of great spiritual and moral strength as well as driving energy. She became the

Treasurer and Administrator of the new movement, and profoundly affected the first fifty years of its life. She personally presented a petition to Charles II on the Quaker commitment to peace, urging the government to be tolerant to Quakers. She was imprisoned for a total of nearly six years for holding Quaker meetings in her home and for refusing to take oaths.

Another courageous early Friend was Mary Fisher. With great determination and courage in 1657 she carried the Quaker message the length of the Mediterranean Sea to the Turkish Emperor Sultan Mohammed IV. She was convinced she had a great truth to share with him. He respected her, listened to her and agreed with what she said as it fitted well with his Muslim views. He ensured she began her return journey home in safety.

John Woolman, like Fox, was a young man with a deep concern to be faithful to the teachings of Jesus. He was the first to challenge slave owning within the Quaker community of New England in North America. With great tact and powerful convictions, he persuaded his fellow Quakers to commit to end slave owning and trading in America.

He travelled through dangerous country to learn from first-nation American peoples the religious insights they had to share and to offer them the insights he had gained from his Quaker experiences. This was a very different approach from the Christian missionaries concerned to impose their beliefs and practices on folk they regarded as heathen. Woolman was so unusually radical that he came to refuse to wear clothes of material that had been dyed because the dyeing process was done by slaves. Initially, all his ideas and practices were often criticised, thought odd, misunderstood and sometimes ridiculed, before the value of those convictions came to be accepted more widely. He came to England to share his message and was at first coldly rejected. His odd appearance did not help. He later died at York, where he is buried. Respect for him grew within the Quaker community here, once his message was understood.

These men and women of conviction, inspired by love and faith, and this vision of the light, challenged the norms of their time. They were singular enough to think differently about the religious teaching and practices common in their day, and proclaim new ways of understanding the message of Jesus and the New Testament.

The scene in Britain today is very different from the 1640s. Then, Christian religious practice and teaching was the shared experience of just about everybody, although there were lots of disagreements between different groups about what should be taught and practiced. Today Christian congregations are clearly a minority, in which the distinctive Quaker voice is a minority within a minority.

Known by our 'fruits'

George Trevelyan in his classic *English Social History* wrote: "The finer essence of George Fox's queer teaching, common to the excited revivalists who were his first disciples, and to the 'quiet' Friends of later times, was surely this – that Christian qualities matter much more than Christian dogmas. No Church or sect had ever made that its living rule before."[7]

How this contrasts with a quotation from *Mansfield Park* – a novel by Jane Austen. In the final chapter of that book, Austen described the two sisters Maria and Julia (after Maria had left her husband for another man and Julia had eloped): "They had been instructed theoretically in their religion, but never required to bring it into daily practice." That observation could apply to many people throughout the Christian generations. Such a disconnect between theory and practice is challenged by the Quaker Way, as it is by all the best Christian formation and training.

Jesus himself said that the test of whether we walk in his way is to be seen in the quality of our lives. "You will be know them by their fruits,"[8] he said in the Sermon on the Mount.[11] The apostle Paul described the fruit of the spirit as: "love, joy, peace, patience, kindness, goodness, trustfulness, gentleness and self-control."[9]

Jesus criticised the hypocrisy of professional religious

people in his own day, and their all too frequent emphasis on strict rules for religious practice, rather than on empathy, compassion, and care.[10] He praised those who were generous and honest.[11] He was compassionate to those who sinned, and encouraged them to change their ways.[12] He said little about sexual relationships but he urged people to love one another. He certainly criticised those who lusted, in their thoughts as well as in their actions.[13]

What the early Quakers made of this is included in these two examples:

Isaac Pennington wrote in 1667: "Our life is love, and peace, and tenderness; and bearing one with another, and forgiving one another, and not laying accusations one against another; but praying one for another and helping one another up with a tender hand."[14]

William Penn wrote in 1682: "True Godliness don't turn men out of the world, but enables them to live better in it, and excites their endeavours to mend it."[15]

In conclusion

This book arose from many discussions over several years of books about Jesus. So much of the information and the insights in these books have helped me and others to engage with Jesus of Nazareth in ways which we have found to be modern, relevant, and spiritual. I hope this perspective on Jesus today will encourage readers who wish to explore further to look into the insights and knowledge in some of the books listed in Appendix 1.

There are different ways of being Quaker. We cherish diversity in unity. What I have described here is one way of being a follower of Jesus of Nazareth. Obviously it is not the only way, or indeed the only way of being Quaker. It has many elements that can enrich the experience of people who are not Quakers, who find this approach appealing.

It includes the exploration of silence as a foundation for spiritual practice as members of a community who share similar values. It emphasises the practical application of threads from Jesus' teaching in modern life. Some people who are Quakers, or attend Quaker meetings, are members of other churches and other faith communities. We Quakers warmly welcome them to participate in our way as well as, and not instead of, their own. One tradition enriches the other.

This understanding of Jesus challenges, encourages and motivates some of us who seek to follow in his way. Many of the artistic representations of Jesus that we are so familiar with, are creations of previous generations. What inspired them was different to what can move us today. The ancient imagery, and traditional hymns and prayers provide a mindset which can limit our perceptions of who Jesus was, and who he can be for us. I found this perspective a real relief and a psychological boost to engage with Jesus today. I hope you may do so too.

In Friendship
Michael Wright

APPENDIX 1

SOME AUTHORS & SOME OF THEIR BOOKS

The story of George Fox and the Quaker Movement is well told in these books:

Ingle, H.L. 1994. *First Among Friends – George Fox and the Creation of Quakerism.* Oxford University Press. ISBN 0-19-510117-0.

Punshon, J. 1984. *Portrait in Grey – a short history of the Quakers.* Quaker Home Service, London. ISBN 0-85245-180-6.

Two slim books by Quakers which tell of current Quaker practice, and understanding of belief, and are helpfully enlightening to Quakers and to those interested to know more about Quakers are:

Durham, G. 2019. *What do Quakers believe?* Christian Alternative Books.

Grant, R. 2019. *Telling the Truth about God.* Christian Alternative Books.

•

Search the web for any of these authors and you will find interesting insights into them and their writings.

Marcus Borg

He writes clearly and simply of who Jesus was and what he means today. His book *Meeting Jesus Again for the First Time* was lent to me by a Friend at my meeting when I began attending in 1998. It initiated my journey of discovery of a fresh appreciation of Jesus. I was very enthused by it. It is a really helpful insight into fresh ways of reading the bible.

Borg, Marcus J.
1996. *Meeting Jesus Again for the First Time: the historical Jesus & the heart of contemporary faith.* San Francisco, CA Harper San Francisco. ISBN 978-0-06-060916-0.
2003. *The Heart of Christianity: Rediscovering a Life of Faith.* San Francisco, CA: Harper San Francisco. ISBN 978-0-06-073068-0. How we can be passionate believers today.
2006. *Jesus: Uncovering the Life, Teachings, and Relevance of a Religious Revolutionary.* San Francisco, CA: Harper San Francisco. ISBN 978-0-06-059445-9.
2017. *Days of Awe and Wonder: how to be a Christian in the twenty-first century.* New York: Harper One. ISBN 978-0-06-245733-2. This is an anthology of his writings about how to be a Christian in the 21st century, gathered by his wife after his death.

Borg, Marcus J & Crossan, John Dominic

2006. *The Last Week: what the gospels really teach about Jesus's final days in Jerusalem.* San Francisco, CA: Harper San Francisco. ISBN 978-0-06-087260-1.

2007. *The First Christmas: What the Gospels Really Teach About Jesus' Birth.* New York: Harper One. ISBN 978-0-06-143070-1.

This pair of books provide excellent introductions to the stories surrounding Jesus' birth, and death.

John Dominic Crossan

He writes of the connection between religion and politics, in the Roman empire and today – citizenship and intelligent faith.

2007. *God & Empire - Jesus against Rome, then and now.* Harper San Francisco, ISBN 978-0-06-084323-6.

John Shelby Spong

Very readable for the non-specialist, Spong has written many books. These are a few which are helpful in understanding Jesus, and his significance for us today.

Spong, J.S.

1988. *This Hebrew Lord.* Harper San Francisco. ISBN 0-06-067520-9. A valuable understanding of Jesus' Hebrew context.

1994. *Resurrection – Myth or Reality?* Harper One. New York. ISBN 978-0-06-6742-9. He explores the accounts of Jesus' death and resurrection, and offers – a controversial – explanation to account for it.

1996. *Liberating the Gospels – reading the gospels with Jewish eyes.* Harper San Francisco. This helps to see why we don't take great sections of the gospels literally.

2001. *A New Christianity for a New World.* Harper San Francisco ISBN 0-06-06708-4. He calls for a radical reformation of the Jesus story.

2007. *Jesus for the Non Religious.* Harper San Francisco. ISBN 978-0-06-076207-0. A helpful modern presentation.

2016. *Biblical Literalism – a Gentile heresy.* Harper One, New York. ISBN 978-0-06-236230-8. A commentary on Matthew's gospel which shows why fundamentalist Christians misunderstand the Hebrew origins of the Bible.

2018. *Unbelievable – Why Neither Ancient Creeds Nor the Reformation Can Produce a Living Faith Today.* Harper One, New York. ISBN 978-0-06-264129-8.

Geza Vermes

He was raised a Roman Catholic and became a priest. He then discovered his Jewish origins, and left Christianity. He has translated the Dead Sea Scrolls and became the first Professor of Jewish Studies in the University of Oxford. He views Jesus from a Jewish perspective which sheds new light on many aspects of his life and ministry. "In Vermes, Jesus has found his best Jewish interpreter," wrote E.P. Sanders.

Vermes, G.

2001. *The Changing Faces of Jesus.* Penguin Books. ISBN 978-0-14-026542-8. In this book he works back from the gospel of John, through the other three gospels, then the Acts of the Apostles and then Paul to show how the picture of Jesus changed over the early years of the Christian church.

2004. *The Authentic Gospel of Jesus.* Penguin Books. ISBN 0-141-00360-X. A search for the original message of Jesus.

2008. *The Resurrection.* Doubleday, USA. ISBN 978-0-385-52242-7. He reviews the various accounts of Jesus' resurrection in the gospels, and offers six possible theories to explain it.

2012. *Christian Beginnings – from Nazareth to Nicaea AD 30-325.* Penguin Books. ISBN 078-0-141-03799-0. He examines all the surviving texts of early Christianity, and traces the evolution of the figure of Jesus from the man he was to the mystery he came to be.

David Boulton

A professional journalist, who was raised in the strict practices of the Plymouth Brethren which he came to reject. He re-discovered his interest in Jesus through the Sea of Faith movement and has produced this comprehensive survey of the search over the last 150 to discover the historical Jesus.

Boulton, D.

2008. *Who on Earth Was Jesus?: The Modern Quest for the Jesus of History.* O Books, Winchester UK & Washington USA. ISBN 978-1-84694-018-7.

Also:

2005. *The Trouble with God: Building the Republic of Heaven.* ISBN 978-1-84694-018-7.

E.P. Sanders

He was a professor of religious studies in Oxford, England; in Duke University, North Carolina; and in Trinity College Dublin.

Sanders, E.P.

1993. *The historical figure of Jesus.* Penguin Books. ISBN 0-14-014499-4. A scholarly presentation of Jesus.

Maurice Casey

He describes himself as an independent historian. He was a Professor of New Testament Language and Literature at the University of Nottingham. He is a scholar with a rare familiarity with both Aramaic and Hebrew, who provides an insight into Jesus background and culture as well as his life and ministry.

Casey, M.

2010. *Jesus of Nazareth – An independent historian's account of his life and teaching.* T & T Clark International. London & New York. ISBN 978-0-567-64517-3.

Reza Aslan

He was raised a Muslim, became an evangelical Christian, reverted to Muslim mystic practice as a Suffi.

Aslan, R.
2013. *Zealot – the life and times of Jesus of Nazareth.* Westbourne Press, London. ISBN 978-1-908906-27-4. He shifts through the myths surrounding Jesus and reveals a complex man who was religious but also a politically conscious revolutionary.
2017. *God – a human history.* Bantam Press. ISBN 978-0-5930-7982-9. A review of 6,000 years of religious practice.

Charles Freeman

He is a historian specialising in the history of ancient Greece and Rome.

Freeman, C.
2002. *The Closing of the Western Mind – The rise of faith and the fall of reason.* Random House. ISBN 0-7126-6498-X. A historian's view of how the formulation of Christian doctrine in the fourth century created a closed-mind in Europe – with the development of opposition between science and religion, Christianity's discomfort with sex, and the development of anti-semitism.
2009. *A New history of Early Christianity.* Yale University Press. ISBN 978-0-300-12581-8.

Lloyd Geering

A New Zealander and Presbyterian, former Professor of Old Testament Studies.

Geering, L.

2002. *Christianity without God.* Bridget Williams Books, New Zealand. ISBN 1-877242-24-1. He sees the modern secular form of Christian culture as a logical consequence of the development of the traditional doctrines. He links modern humanism to the Wisdom literature of the Old Testament.

Karen Armstrong

A former Catholic nun, she has become a world-renowned scholar of religion, and written biographies of the Buddha, Mohammed, and many other books.

Armstrong, K.

2007. *The Bible – The biography.* Atlantic Books, London. ISBN 978-1-84354-396-1. A very readable history of the development of the Bible.

1993. *A History of God.* Random House. The 4,000 year story of the quest for God by the Hebrews, Christian, Muslims, mystics, reformers, and through the enlightenment to the "death of God".

APPENDIX 2
REFERENCES

Chapter 1
A fresh engagement with Jesus

1. *Quaker faith & practice* 19.02
2. Matthew 25. 31-46
3. John 8. 2-11
4. Matthew 22.15-22
5. Mathew 6.1-8 & Luke 11.37-44
6. John 4. 1-42
7. Luke 8.1-3
8. Matthew 7.1-5
9. Matthew 19.24
10. *Quaker faith & practice: The book of Christian discipline of the Yearly Meeting of the Religious Society of Friends (Quakers) in Britain* (ISBN 978-1-907123-55-9) is, as I noted at the end of my Introduction *What's this all about?* The handbook for Quakers on the practice of the Quaker way.
11. *Quaker faith & practice* 26.09
12. *Quaker faith & practice* 26: 41
13. *Quaker faith & practice* 26: 43
14. *Quaker faith & practice* 26:50
15. *Quaker faith & practice* 26:53

16. Matthew 4.25

17. Mark 1.35

18. John 1.9 and *Quaker faith & practice* 19.07

19. Darwin, Charles. *On the Origin of Species by means of Natural Selection*. Philadelphia: University of Pennsylvania Press, 1959 originally published 1859.

20. Spong, John Shelby. *Unbelievable*. Harper Collins, New York. 2018, pages 46-47

21. Aslan, Reza. *God*. Bantam Press. London 2017, page 170

22. Spong, John Shelby. *Unbelievable*. Harper Collins, New York. 2018, pages 65-66

23. Mark 14.36

Chapter 2
Growing in light and love

1. Mark 1.12-13; Matthew 4.1-11; Luke 4.1-13

2. Mark 1.35

3. Matthew 26.36-46

4. Mark 6.31

5. Matthew 6. 5-13

6. 1 Kings 19.1-12

7. Revelation 8.1

8. *Quaker faith & practice* 2.18

9. *Quaker faith & practice* 20.11

10. *Advices & Queries* 28

11. *Advices & Queries* 8

12. Dawes, Joycelin. *Discernment and Inner Knowing.* FeedARead.com Publishing, 2017, pages 80-82

13. Acts of the Apostles 9.2; 18.26; 19.9; 22.04; 24.14 & 22

14. Manocha, Ramesh. *Silence Your Mind.* Orion, London. 2014 ISBN 978-1-4091-5394-8 and his website www.beyondthemind.com

15. Sheldrake, Philip. *Spirituality – a very short introduction.* Oxford University Press. 2012

16. Holley, Brian. *Why Silence?* Brian Holley. The Kindlers Booklet 12. 2016

17. Wall, Ginny. *Deepening the life of the Spirit.* Quaker Books. 2012

18. Wall, Ginny. *Becoming Friends.* Quaker Life & Woodbrooke Quaker Study Centre. 2010 pages 266-275.

19. Matthew 6.25-34

20. Poem: *Leisure* – W.H. Davies

21. John Matthew 7.3

22. *Advices & Queries* 17

23. *Quaker faith & practice* 21.15

Chapter 3
Some elements of the Quaker way

1. *Advices & Queries* 1

2. Fox, George. *The Journal.* p14 chapter for the year 1646-7. Penguin. 1998

3. Jeremiah 31.33-34

4. Joel 2.28-32 and Acts 2.17-21

5. Fox, George. *The Journal.* p14 chapter for the year 1646-7. Penguin. 1998.

6. See pages 209-212 in Punshon, John. *Portrait in Grey, a short history of the Quakers.* Quaker Home Service, London. 1984.

7. Ambler, Rex. *The Quaker Way – a rediscovery.* Christian Alternative, Winchester. 2012.

8. www.theguardian.com/news/2018/aug/27/religion-why-is-faith-growing-and-what-happens-next *How many believers are there around the world.* Harriet Sherwood.

9. *Becoming a Quaker diversity and inclusion ally* by Nim Njuguna, published in the Friends Quarterly, volume forty-seven number one, February 2019.

10. *Owning power & privilege.* A Toolkit for Action produced by Quakers in Britain.

11. *Becoming a Quaker diversity and inclusion ally* by Nim Njuguna, published in the Friends Quarterly, volume forty-seven number one, February 2019.

12. *Quaker faith & practice* 19.07

Chapter 4
A Quaker approach to the bible

1. Luke 10.35-37

2. Luke 15.11-32

3. Amos 5.14, 15, & 21-24

4. Isaiah 1.17

5. see Leviticus chapter 25 and Deuteronomy chapter. 15, Exodus 22 and Deuteronomy 23 for examples of an ideal of social justice.

6. Leviticus 19. 17-18

7. *Quaker faith & practice* 19.24, and 27. 30 -34 I find particularly helpful.

8. Armstrong, Karen. *The Bible – the biography*. Atlantic Books, London. 2007. Chapter entitled 'Midrash'.

9. The Book of Common Prayer of the Church of England – 1662 – Oxford University Press. The Apostles' creed is in both Morning and Evening Prayer, the Nicean creed is in The Communion Service, and the creed of St. Athanasius comes immediately after Evening Prayer and is entitled: Quicunque Vult.

10. Freeman, Charles. *The Closing of the Western Mind – the rise of faith and the fall of reason.* Random House, UK. 2003.

11. *Owning power & privilege* – a toolkit for action from Britain Yearly Meeting 2019.

12. Matthew 5.1-12

13. Vosper, Greta. *With or Without God*. Harper Collins, 2008 paperback p255.

14. Matthew 7.12 & Luke 6.31

15. Luke 3.1-20

16. Matthew 14.12

17. Mark 1.15

18. Daniel 7.13,14

19. *Advices & Queries* number 2

20. Matthew 13.33 & Luke 13.21

21. *Advices & Queries* number 4

Chapter 5
The Jesus books

1.   Fox, George. *The Journal*. Chapter for 1656.
Penguin. 1998.

2.   Daniel chapter 3 verse 21.

3.   Armstrong, Karen. *The Bible – the biography*.
Atlantic Books, London. 2007.

4.   Ezra chapters 3-5

5.   Meyer, Marvin. *The Secret Gospels of Jesus*. Darton
Longman & Todd, London. 2007.

6.   https://en.wikipedia.org/wiki/New_Testament_
Apocrypha

7.   Crossan, John Dominic. *God & Empire – Jesus
against Rome then and now*. Harper San Francisco 2007.
Page 23.

MARK

8.   Evans, Craig A. in *Mark – Commentary on the Bible*,
edited by James D.G. Dunn and John W. Rogerson.
Erdmans, Grand Rapids USA, 2003. Page 1066.

9.   Mark 11.13-26

10. Mark 10.35-40

11. Mark 8.22-30

12. Mark 5.1-20

13. Mark 1.1

14. Evans, Craig A. in *Mark – Commentary on the Bible*, edited by James D.G. Dunn and John W. Rogerson. Erdmans, Grand Rapids USA 2003. Page 1066.

15. Mark 1.1-8

16. Vermes, Geza. *Christian Beginnings – from Nazareth to Nicaea AD 30-325.* Penguin Books, 2013. Chapter 2 *The Charismatic Religion of Jesus.*

17. Mark 4.1-9

18. Mar 4.21-23

19. Mark 4.30-32

20. Mark 5.1-20

21. Mark 11.15-19

22. Mark 15.23-47.

23. Mark 16.8 and 16.9-20

MATTHEW

24. Acts 11.26

25. Matthew 23.13-15

26. Matthew 27.25

27. Matthew 1.1-17

28. Genesis chapter 38

29. The book of Ruth chapters 2-4

30. Second Book of Samuel chapters 11 & 12

31. Matthew 1.18-25

32. Joshua chapters 2-6

33. Matthew 2.13-23

34. Exodus chapters 1-15

35. Matthew chapter 3

36. Matthew 4.1-11

37. Isaiah 8.23 – 9.1

38. Matthew 7.28; 11.1; 13.53; 19.1; 16.1

39. Matthew chapters 5-7

40. Matthew chapter 10

41. Matthew chapter 13

42. Matthew chapter 18

43. Matthew chapters 24 & 25

44. Matthew chapters 26 & 27

45. Matthew chapter 28

46. Spong, J.S. *Biblical Literalism – a Gentile heresy*
Harper. New York. 2016.

LUKE

47. Luke 1.1-4

48. Luke 2.1-20

49. Luke 2.22-28

50. Bach, David L. in *Luke in Eerdmanns Commentary on the Bible*. Eerdmans, Grand Rapids, Michigan. 2003, page 1106.

51. Luke 1.5-2.38

52. Luke 3.1-22

53. Luke 3.23-38

54. Luke 4.1-30

55. Luke 6.20-49

JOHN

76. John 9.1-41

77. John 11.1-54

78. John 10.1-21

79. John 8.12 & 9.5

80. John 6.35

81. John 10.36

82. John 15.1

83. John 11.25

84. John chapters 13-17

85. John 13.34-35

86. Spong, J.S. *The Fourth Gospel: Tales of a Jewish Mystic.* Harper One. 2013.

87. John 1.29 & 45

88. Compare: Mark 1.16-20; Matthew 4.18-22; Luke 5.1-11; John 1.35-51

89. John 2.1-11

90. John 2.13-22

91. John 12.36

92. John 1.11

93. John 18.25-27

94. John 19.25-27

95. 11.35

96. John 4.6

97. Spong, J.S. *The Fourth Gospel: Tales of a Jewish Mystic.* Harper One. 2013.

Chapter 6
Revising our understanding of the Jesus story

1. Luke 10.23-37
2. John 8.3-11 Most translations have a note nearby to explain that these verses were not part of the earliest manuscripts, but was added later by a different editor.
3. Matthew 20.1-16
4. *Advices & Queries* 22
5. Genesis 17.17 & 21.1-7
6. I Samuel chapter 1
7. Luke 1.5-25 & 57-80
8. Exodus 1.8 -2.10
9. Matthew chapter 2
10. Borg, Marcus J. & Crossan, John Dominic. *The First Christmas — what the gospels really teach about Jesus' birth.* Harper One, New York. 2007. This is a very readable book which explores this scenario in detail.
11. Exodus 13.17 – 15.21
12. Joshua chapter 3
13. 2 Kings 2.7 – 14
14. Mark 4.37 – 41 & 6.48-52
15. Exodus chapter 16
16. Mark 6.35-44; Matthew 14.13-21; Luke 9. 12-17; John 6.5-13. and Mark 8.1-8; Matthew 15.32-38
17. First book of Kings chapter 17 – Second Book of Kings chapter 2.
18. I Kings 19.1-13

19. II Kings 2.8

20. II Kings chapter 4

21. Acts of the Apostles 1.6-11

22. Luke 7.11-15

23. John 11.1-44

24. Spong, J.S. *Unbelievable*. Harper One, New York. 2018.

25. Casey, Maurice. *Jesus of Nazareth – an independent historian's account of his life and teaching*. T & T Clark – London, 2010. Chapter 12: Did Jesus rise from the dead?

26. Borg, Marcus J. & Crossan, John Dominic. *The Last Week – a day by day account of Jesus's final week in Jerusalem*. Harper. San Francisco. 2006: chapter 8 Easter Sunday.

27. Ibid – page 207.

28. Vermes, Geza. *The Resurrection*. Doubleday, New York, 2008: final chapter Epilogue.

29. Mark 13.19

30. Luke 21.5-28

31. Matthew chapter 24

32. Borg, Marcus J. & Crossan, John Dominic. *The Last Week – a day by day account of Jesus's final week in Jerusalem*. Harper San Francisco. 2006: chapter 8 Easter Sunday.

33. Crossan, John Dominic. *God & Empire – Jesus against Rome, then and now*. Harper San Francisco. 2007.

34. Revelation 17.1-7

35. Revelation 21.1-8

36. Matthew 12.10-13

37. Matthew 9.27-31

38. Mark 7.31-37

39. Luke 17.11-19

40. Mark 1.1-12

41. see Vermes, Geza. *Jesus the Jew*. SCM Press. 1973. Chapter 1.

42. see Sharman, Cecil. *George Fox & the Quakers*. Quaker books London. 1991. Chapter 12.

Chapter 7
Some Quaker responses to Jesus

1. *Quaker faith & practice* 19.02

2. Fox, George. *The Journal*. Chapter for 1648.

3. John 1.9

4. Fox, George. *The Journal*. Chapter for 1650.

5. Fox, George. *The Journal*. Chapter for 1649.

6. *The Revelation of John*. Chapter 4-6, & 13 &14.

7. Trevelyan, G.M. *English Social History*. William Clowes, London. 1944.

8. Matthew 7.15-20

9. Galatians 5.22

10. Matthew chapter 23

11. Luke 21.1-4

12. John 8.1-11

13. Matthew 5.27-28

14. *Quaker faith & practice* 10.01

15. *Quaker faith & practice* 21.17